# Ghana

Christine Leonard

New Wine Press

New Wine Ministries,
P.O. Box 17,
Chichester,
West Sussex PO20 6YB
England





ISBN 0 947852 55 7

Printed in England by Clays Ltd, St Ives plc

Typeset by Alpha Typesetting, 17 New Road, Chatham, Kent

# Contents

# Foreword

In the history of world mission there are all too few pioneers, men and women who, against all the odds and pressures to give up, obey God and go forward. Men like Hudson Taylor and C. T. Studd. I believe James McKeown was such a man.

James was raised on a farm in Northern Ireland and went to Ghana with his wife Phia, and in 53 years saw 3,500 churches established.

It was my privilege to meet James on several occasions and I was always moved by his willingness to learn, even in old age, and especially from me, a much younger man. In my few meetings with James I learned so much, though knowing James, he was probably unaware of it, such was the humility of the man. He believed and practised the exhortion of Scripture which says "In honour, preferring one another." (Romans 12:10 AV).

It was always difficult to get James to talk of his exploits. He was fearful and careful that only God should get the glory and constantly remarked "I have built nothing."

This book has taken a good deal of research by Christine. Fortunately there were extensive records kept of all the executive meetings, and several people who had been with James from the beginning were still alive and available.

This account of the life and work of James will thrill, challenge and inspire you. In the light of the current move of God's Spirit in the Church to reach out and evangelise the world, Christine has written a timely book. This is a story of a man who took risks for God; James's only desire was to please Him!

May this book, as you read it, challenge you to do the same.

NORMAN BARNES
*(Director of Links International)*

# Preface

This book really started when John, my husband, went to a meeting where Norman Barnes introduced two Ghanaians from the Church of Pentecost. John was impressed. "They're speaking tomorrow night," he told me, "Go and take notes. It might make an article." I went and listened to them open-mouthed, as they told the story of how James McKeown started their mushrooming church in West Africa. "That's not an article – that's a book," I joked to John on returning home, but somehow, the thought would not go away.

Africa invaded our front room with TV images that were always bad news – war, famine, poverty, disease. Yet I had heard good news, amazing news coming out of Africa – news the church in the UK needed to hear, news to bring hope that God is on the move.

James McKeown, retired and living in Northern Ireland, insisted he did not want to be interviewed – "Why should anyone write a book about me, I've done nothing." What could I say if he was determined that establishing one of the fastest growing churches around was "nothing"?

A year went by and I had almost forgotten about the whole thing when the phone rang. "This is David Mills," said a voice. David explained that he had worked with James in Ghana for many years and thought he could arrange an interview. "How soon can you be in Northern Ireland?" he wanted to know.

June 1986 found me in James's front room, at the beginning of a day and a half's conversation about his life and work. There was so much to take in! One thing became clear – James was an extraordinary man of God! I felt privileged to have heard him and all the more determined his story should not be forgotten. James lent me a book written and published privately by his brother Adam, which gave much information I would otherwise have missed.

Before I left, James said, "One day you'll go to Ghana and see it all for yourself!" I smiled politely, thanking God for my two young children. Ghana was the last place on earth I wanted to visit and surely it is unreasonable to expect an unadventurous Surrey housewife to abandon her children in favour of researching books in tropical Africa ... isn't it?

The Church of Pentecost was preparing a short history of itself, which I was able to study in its draft form. I scoured the country for other material. The story was becoming more exciting than I had imagined possible. One morning, to my horror, I woke up realising that, despite the practical difficulties, the heat and the creepy crawlies, I *did* want to go to Ghana and see it all for myself. After the initial shock, my husband was supportive. I phoned the leader of my church. "Martin, I want to go to Ghana," I announced, half expecting him to rush round and pray that I be restored to my right mind. Instead, his reply mystified me. "Oh yes," he said, "Have you had a letter?" I had not. "Norman Barnes wrote to me today," explained Martin, "asking if anyone from our church would like to go on a team he is taking to Ghana. He's taking twelve people from this country to help the Church of Pentecost celebrate their jubilee. It's fifty years since James landed in Accra." It was decided that Martin and I should go and my friend Jayne Lindsell should also come to help me with the research.

By this time I knew perhaps too much about Ghana and I was terrified. In actual fact we spent a superb three weeks there, over Easter 1987, cared for by the Church of Pentecost in a way we shall never forget. Jayne and I stayed in Accra and were able to visit Kumasi and the Akwapim hills. David Mills supplied us with a list of people we should try to interview, though we had no idea where most of these were located. We saw many prayers answered in Ghana, not least that we were able to meet and have lengthy conversations with many who had been pioneers in the Church with James.

We also had access to Church minutes and other documents which proved invaluable. A few months later, I went with my husband to stay with James in Northern Ireland and was able to fill in still more details from our conversations at that time.

So I would like to say a big "Thank you":
to James McKeown and the Church of Pentecost, especially to Pastor A T Nartey, who unwittingly started me on this project;
to David and Margaret Mills, Norman and Grace Barnes, Martin Scott, Gerald Coates, Jayne Lindsell and Rod Boreham for all their encouragement and help;
to my husband, children, family and friends who helped in so many practical ways:
to the people who helped me gather material – Cecil and Jean Cousen, the Cawthornes, Malcolm and Barbara Cummins, Bobby Mearns, Pastor and Mrs McCandless and Pearl in the UK, to Adam McKeown in the USA and in Ghana to the Revs F. S. Safo, M. K. Yeboah, L. A. Nyarko, Apau Asante, F. D. Walker, Opoku Onyinah and Kwame Noble Atsu; to Pastor and Mrs E. O. Ofori, Mrs Eunice Addison, Mrs Esme Siriboe, Mrs Victoria Vanderpuije, Mrs Mary Adams, Miss Adelaide Koram and to Elders Johnny Mallet, E. K. Danquah and K. L. Odame-Otoo.

## A few words of explanation about names.

I asked James what I should call him in this book. In Ghana, he was referred to as 'Pastor McKeown', or, as they pronounced it, 'Pastor McQueue'. To those who knew him better he was 'Pastor James.' In the UK most people just called him 'James' and this is how he wanted to be known in the book.

Ghana gained independence in 1957. For the first twenty years of this story, her people should properly be known as, 'The natives of the Gold Coast.' James called them 'Africans' and so have I. After Independence they are Ghanaians.

The church James founded also changed its name. In an attempt to avoid confusion, for the purposes of this book I have called it the Church with a capital C.

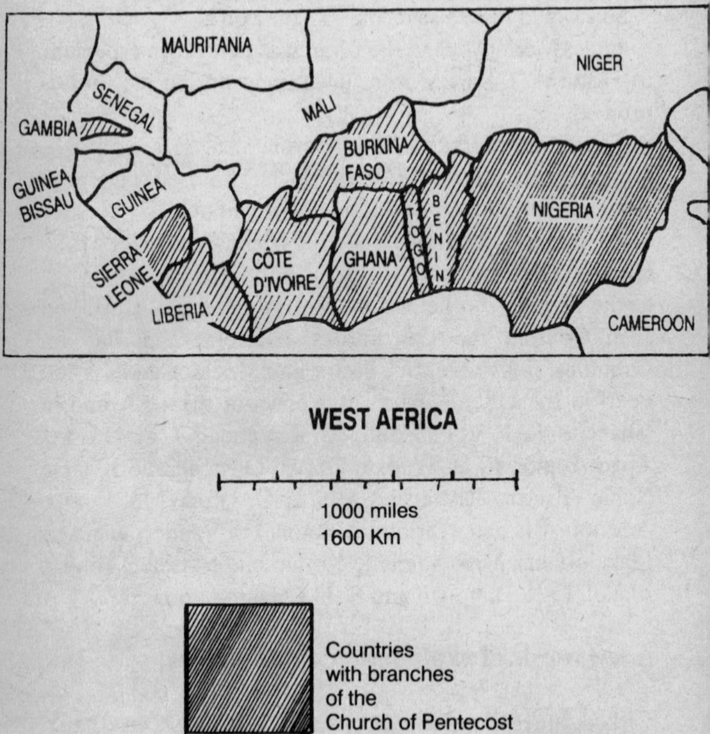

# Map of Ghana

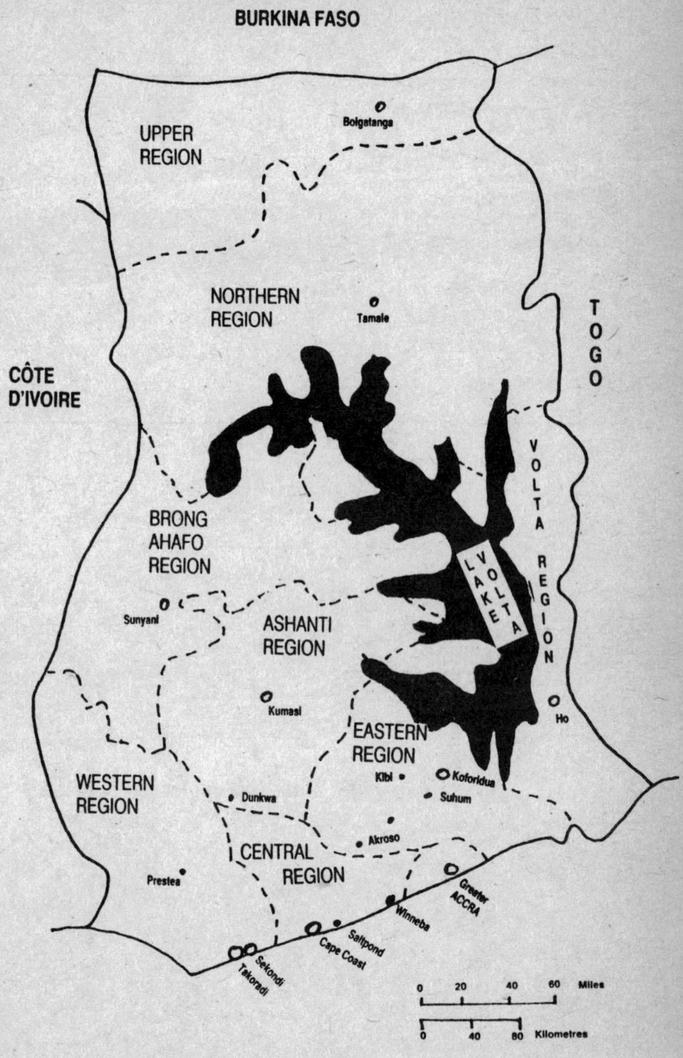

BURKINA FASO
UPPER REGION
Bolgatanga
NORTHERN REGION
Tamale
TOGO
CÔTE D'IVOIRE
BRONG AHAFO REGION
VOLTA
LAKE VOLTA
VOLTA REGION
Sunyani
ASHANTI REGION
Kumasi
Ho
EASTERN REGION
Kibi
Koforidua
Suhum
WESTERN REGION
Dunkwa
Akroso
CENTRAL REGION
Prestea
Greater ACCRA
Winneba
Saltpond
Cape Coast
Sekondi
Takoradi
0 20 40 60 Miles
0 40 80 Kilometres

# The Seed that Splits Rocks

*"As I look back, one supreme thought rises in my mind: why should a man of God ever have an anxious thought? Why can't he prepare the ground, sow the seed, eat, drink and sleep and leave that silent power of nature to do her own work? I feel deeply conscious of what one has called "unconscious blasphemy" – lack of faith in the creative power of the Word of God. It must grieve the heart of God to see His servants with whom He has entrusted the power of His eternal Word, worrying about difficulties, pushing for results, interfering with that seed which can split rocks, open graves, unlock prison doors, give sight to the blind, hearing to the deaf, speech to the dumb and strength to the lame. Oh the limitless power of that Word.*

*"In spite of all difficulties, the eternal Word germinated, the blade appeared, then were our hearts glad. Planted by Pauls, watered by Apollos', God gave the increase. What was once a seed hidden away in the dark clods has now become a large tree, having fruit, bearing branches; and even at this stage the call is for more faith.*

*"Eight years ago, how comforting were the words, 'Can these bones live?' The call was for faith in the Word. When the tender life did appear, "Can it survive?" was the question. God is good, the tree has grown; from the branches there hangs fruit. But there are still birds in the air and they want a place to nest. There are still snakes in the grass and they want the little birds, so they have to climb the tree. There are many insects – they want the fruit. There are diseases carried by the insects who feed on the life of the fruit. 'Can God preserve and keep that which has been planted from all these evils?' "*

James McKeown, writing in 1945 as quoted in *History of the Church of Pentecost (West Africa)* (Church of Pentecost: Accra, 1987).

# Chapter 1
# The Church of Pentecost Today

Dogs in the compound barked as some heavy glass and wood doors in the house swung open. A man wearing a lightweight grey suit and straw hat stood in the doorway. He was over six feet tall, with powerful shoulders and such an upright bearing he might have been mistaken for a retired soldier.

The man walked into the car port where he stooped to unlock a pale blue Peugeot 504, then drove out through heavy iron gates. Having passed the West German Embassy, the Peugeot began bumping and grinding its way through Ghana's capital city, Accra. Though it was early on Easter Sunday morning, the streets were busy. The man had fleeting impressions of colour and singing as people cheerfully pushed and jostled their way into churches of every kind.

After a couple of miles, the traffic jammed solid. A policeman in shorts standing under some mango trees at the junction tried to free a passage across the link road. The man in the Peugeot resigned himself for a long wait. So many people were converging on his destination, he knew they would make slow progress from now on. Horns blared, engines boiled over. For a moment the man's mind flashed to Easter at home – to sharp sunny mornings and drifts of daffodils bending to the wind. People had hurried to church in County Antrim, too, but not on this scale.

A ramshackle lorry sprouting brown arms and legs pushed by. Loud singing from forty voices within stopped abruptly when someone recognised the man in the Peugeot. "Papa, papa," he cried. "Pastor, Pastor!" echoed the rest of the lorry load, all pushing to hang off the edge so that they too could wave. The man smiled and waved back. Soon he could see crowds several deep at the side of the road, jammed between the traffic and an open sewer. They were all carrying Bibles and waving at him, "Pastor, Pastor!"

They were all converging on a great open-air convention. The man could hear it already. They had started singing early as usual, before anyone had arrived to lead them. Probably many had been here for hours, in order to secure good seats. A palm branch canopy shaded the convention. It had taken months to erect on playing fields behind the Salvation Army school. Only the previous Wednesday, the man had stood in front of the school's mud and wattle buildings and rusting corrugated iron roofs. "The canopy is far too big," he had argued, "whatever are you thinking of?" How wrong he had been! The canopy was, in fact, too small. The man frowned. Any latecomers would have to stand in the full sun.

Eventually the man found his parking space round the back of the platform. He peeled himself off the car seat, wiped the sweat from his hands and neck and joined a hundred or so other pastors on the platform. Like him, they all wore suits and ties or clerical collars. He looked around. The crowd, 80,000 strong, were packed tightly in an area which he estimated to be as big as a football ground back home. There had been so much to think of, to organise, and now it seemed the Church of Pentecost had even succeeded in bringing the city's traffic to a standstill. No wonder everyone was asking, "Who are these people, who can attract such crowds?"

The man watched the sandy square in front of the platform where the women had just been dancing and where a number of deaconesses were sprinkling water in an attempt to settle the fog of dust. Then they returned to their seats to the right of the square near the pastor's wives. Behind them, seated on wooden benches, rows of women stretched so far their faces were indistinguishable, the bright colours of their clothes a blur.

In the distance, behind them, were stalls which had sprung up all round the edge of the meeting place like a temporary village. They catered for the needs of the great crowd that was now assembled here for the sixth time in four days. Bibles were sold, but so were canned drinks, fried yam, fried plantain, pepper stew and *kenke,*[1] wrapped in banana leaves. A spicy smell drifted from great cauldrons bubbling over charcoal fires and tickled the man's nose.

To the left of the sandy square sat elders and deacons and behind them, the other men of the Church, some with their traditional cloth draped over one dark shoulder, some in more casual European clothes. Facing the pastors across the square the drummers were playing for all they were worth and two or three rows of women with *akasa* – tambourines – joined in unison. To one side were two guitars and a big double bass with just a couple of strings. A perspiring song-leader beat time as he yelled into one of the microphones at the front of the platform.

Sunlight dappled through the browning palm branch canopy onto 80,000 Africans, all singing and twirling their white hankies in the air in praise of Jesus. They had travelled here not only from near and far within Ghana itself, but from several other West African countries. Many had made great sacrifices in order to be able to attend these meetings over the four day Easter holiday. The man knew their nights were none too comfortable, sleeping on the floor of Accra's city schools. The year had been one of drought and exceptional heat and even at this early hour the temperature approached a hundred degrees. The Africans themselves were complaining and the hospitals were full of people with malaria and skin lesions made worse by the weather.

Thinking of these things, the man felt a great wave of emotion sweep over him, so it took him by surprise when the Church's second in command, Pastor Paintsil turned to him and announced, "And now our beloved Founder, Pastor James McKeown, will speak to us."

1 Boiled, fermented corn

The man rose from the chairman's upholstered arm-chair, shed his grey jacket and stood in his short-sleeved white shirt and dark tie, looking out over the crowds. At first he said nothing, he felt too happy. "I was brought up so humble," he thought, "and now I am privileged to speak to a company of people like this!" His mind travelled back through time to a little town further along the coast and he smiled. "To think – when I first gathered the Church, back in 1939, all of us together numbered just 200! How much God has done in less than forty years!"

He had first landed in Accra in 1937, a pioneer missionary with little education and no training. He had come to evangelise a country which was then a British colony – the Gold Coast, but the only thing it had in common with the British Isles was that it covered almost exactly the same area. Now it was 1978 and for forty-one years he had made his home in this tropical land along with ten million Africans from their various tribes. During that time, the seed of the Gospel he had planted had grown and faltered and grown again. He liked to think of the Church as a fine young tree, but early on some of its "branches" became diseased and had to be cut off. Open and hidden attacks on it had been virulent. Tears came into James's eyes... he had come to Africa with nothing but a vision, and the odds against it being fulfilled had seemed so great... yet the Church he planted could no longer be described as a tree. God had given the increase until it was more like an ever-spreading forest.

James had seen other changes too. From a personal point of view he had come through extreme poverty and hardship. Several times he had been near to death. Now he lived in the 'Chairman's Residence' next door to diplomats and ambassadors and his only sadness was that his dear wife's health no longer allowed her to live in Africa. He had broken down barriers between himself and the Africans and he had weathered betrayal from some who were closest to him. These days people in the Church were so devoted to their

'Pastor James' it was almost embarrassing.

There had been great changes in the country, as well. In 1957, Ghana came to Independence under Prime Minister Kwame Nkrumah, the first nation south of the Sahara to do so. James had observed the young nation's struggle with the legacy of colonialism – the British had made its economy prosperous, but had organised it around one crop – cocoa – for which the West was now free to name its price. James had seen a succession of military coups and civilian governments attempt to control the economy, while the country's infrastructure – roads, railways, ports, telephones – deteriorated. Increasingly it seemed Ghana's currency, the cedi, had little value in the outside world.

Still, James had grown to love these Africans. Even if they lived in a poor conditions, surrounded by the ever-present red dust, their clothes were clean and pressed, they walked tall, smiled often and were remarkably creative at finding ways of earning money. He felt there was something special about the people of Ghana and certainly, the pride they felt in their own country seemed to transcend most tribal animosity. Ghanaians were full of fun and laughter and energy. They enjoyed life but they also radiated a simple dignity. They seemed to understand, thought James, that people are more important than things. A system of extended families meant the weak were cared for and no-one was an outcast. Identity-crises and self-doubts plagued many he met in the UK, but these did not seem to be among Ghana's problems. When someone back in England had asked what it was like to be back in civilisation he was genuinely puzzled, for he felt he had left it behind in Africa.

Now here he was, 77 years old and the head of West Africa's fastest-growing evangelical church – not that church growth in itself was hard in a land where everyone believed in spiritual realities. The only question was – which god to follow? New churches were forever springing up, even if many of them were scarcely recognisable as Christian. 600

denominations were registered in one city alone. But most others had either diverged into various weird excesses or remained carbon copies of their American or European roots. James smiled. Certainly there were ways in which the Church of Pentecost was similar to an Elim church back home, but there was one very important difference – it was entirely governed, run and financed by Africans. That had been his dream from the beginning and here it was, on this Easter morning, quite literally spread out before him.

James looked at the two Africans who were to translate his words into Ga and Twi and cast a glance at the loudspeakers wired to thick bamboo poles further back, which other interpreters would use to carry his message into some of the other 57 dialects of this country. Then he began to preach the word God had given him.

. . . . . . . . . . . .

I was there in 1987 as the Church of Pentecost celebrated the fifty years since James first landed in Accra. In half a century, the Church grew from nothing to a membership of 270,000, from no local church to a network of 3,000, covering almost every town and village in Ghana. It continues to grow and opens an average of five new assemblies a week throughout the country.

In Accra I met a WEC missionary and his wife. In the early 1970s, they stayed with James for a week. For one of the very few times in his life, James talked non-stop of how he had built the Church of Pentecost and why he had made certain decisions. This missionary said he had tried to base the rest of his own ministry on all he learned in that week. He has lectured in Bible schools all over the world on the principles James taught him. "People in the Church of Pentecost will tell you the Church has grown because of the Holy Spirit," he said. "Speaking as an outsider, I can see that is true, but it would never have mushroomed in the way it did without

James seeing many principles of Church growth, long before anyone else ever thought of writing books about it. Other churches have expanded until they reached a plateau at a certain size, but so far – just – the Church of Pentecost has managed to keep pace with its growth. The way James caused it to operate is bound to produce growth and a leadership who are trained."

This book, the story of one man's faithfulness to God, will give some clues as to why the Church he founded grows in the way it does. The most obvious reason for growth is that their top priority has always been evangelism. James saw to that. Every member counts sharing their faith as their own responsibility – not just the leaders.

In addition the Church of Pentecost sends out full-time missionaries, both within Ghana, where they now have an assembly in almost every town and village, and abroad. Today the Church of Pentecost is also to be found in the Côte d'Ivoire, Liberia and the Gambia to the west; Burkina Faso to the north; and Togo, Benin and Nigeria to the east. They also have a foothold in Sierra Leone. Their goal is no less than to reach the whole of Africa for Christ.

Another reason for growth is prayer – they are a praying church. One Wednesday morning, when I was in Ghana, I happened to be next door to a building where hundreds of women gather. I heard them pray for over four hours without stopping. At about half past four on most mornings, we would hear members singing on the way to their local assembly's early morning prayer meeting. When they announce a topic for prayer, "Let us pray" means just that – they all pray at once, out loud, with all their might. Power, faith and expectancy are in that prayer. Far from dying away into embarrassed silence, the sound intensity increases until the leader calls a halt and introduces a fresh topic. These people have learnt what it is to gain victory in spiritual warfare. In a country where so many live in fear of evil spirits, and no-one doubts the reality of the battle in heavenly places, they are used to seeing Satan flee before the name of Jesus.

The Church also grows because of its giving. At every meeting, when it is time for the offering, the people dance up to pour their money into plastic washing-up bowls. This can take up to 45 minutes! All during the meeting, individuals come as they are touched by God and put still more money in the bowls. Even in the famine of 1983, when they were eating perhaps once every other day, the giving did not diminish.

Their giving has proved a key to growth and expansion on a scale we only dream of. They are totally self-sufficient financially; the only outside help they receive is from organisations like Elim and Norman Barnes' 'Links International', for the foreign exchange needed to buy a printing-press, parts for vehicles and so on. This is only because the economic situation of the country permits no other alternative. Otherwise, their 700 buildings, their 300 salaries, and their giving to alleviate social hardship in Ghana, all comes from their own funds.

These people have learnt what it is to rely on God for their daily bread and to see His provision. One of our team wanted to give a present to his interpreter, but felt rather mean as the only thing he had with him was a second-hand towel. The interpreter was almost in tears, "For months I have been praying for a towel," he said, "You see, I travel often in my work for the Church but my family only has one towel and I cannot take that."

The main reason the Church has grown is that its people love Jesus – they have been set on fire for Him. It shows in their worship and in their lives. The Church has never allowed compromise – they treat sin and reversion to cultic religious practices as seriously as each one takes his responsibility to Jesus Christ and the Church. In meetings, whenever my interpreter spoke about Jesus and what He had done, a smile illuminated her face and she communicated more than a translation of the preacher's words – something of her joy in the Lord overflowed. When we interviewed some of the Church pioneers and full-time pastors, we almost felt as if we had been talking to Timothy and Titus, Priscilla and Aquila. We were moved by all they had gone through for the sake of the Gospel, by their courage, integrity and wholeheartedness, by their faith to see things through, and by their love which immediately broke down all barriers between us. Also, there was something about each of them which reminded me of James – a strange mix of humility and authority and of peace with God.

. . . . . . . . . . . .

"Why ever have you come all this way to talk to an old man like me?" James wanted to know, when I first met him in 1986. He had retired to Northern Ireland, where he was hardly known. Born in 1900, he left school at 11, helped on his father's farm and later became a tram driver. At the age of 37 he went to the Gold Coast and the Church's story began.

In his bungalow in Ballymena I found a clean-shaven man, with short, stubbly hair, a distinctive slope to his high forehead and a warm smile. Photographs show James tall, upright and strongly built, though he walked with a stick when I met him. He spoke beautifully, choosing each word with care and though he had a soft Scottish accent, often phrased things in a very African way. Whether speaking or silent, he radiated peace. Characteristically, he was more interested in asking about my family than in talking about himself.

James was very reluctant for a book to be written, "I never founded anything – I never opened a single assembly." This is strange as there were hourly bulletins in Ghana's national media when he died in 1989, the Church of Pentecost celebrate their 'Founder's Birthday' and talk of him constantly. He hated all the fuss! He avoided talking about his work in Ghana and much has been lost to the Church world-wide. Those few who do know something of his story insist he was of the calibre of Hudson Taylor or C. T. Studd and that the principles he discovered and made work, could be applied to situations all over the world.

Others have written and theorized about Church growth, James McKeown grew the Church, or rather, Jesus within him did. A quiet, shy, humble, poorly educated man, "yet few others would have stood the test," insisted some of the Ghanaians who knew him best. His life, his accomplishments, his walk with God – they are inspiring. Many of the Ghanaians caught his spirit and "went on to do mightier things". My prayer is that people reading this book may catch that same spirit and be encouraged to hear and obey the voice of God. Who knows what may result?

# Chapter 2
# Beginnings

The fastest growing evangelical church in West Africa was founded in 1938, not through the hundred years of work already done by the established missionary societies in the Gold Coast, but by a single farmer-turned-tram-driver. Perhaps James's secret was that he had no-one to rely on but God. After all, Jesus had no formal training for His ministry – only 30 quiet years during which He learnt to hear and obey His Father.

Long ago, James's parents ran away from their families in Northern Ireland and caught the ferry to Scotland. Having married, they settled in a village called Glenboig, near Glasgow. There in 1898, Jeannie, was born and James followed on September 12th, 1900. The family then moved closer to the city, to Coatbridge, where, in the space of 11 years, came Thomas, William-John, Samuel, Adam and David. Between having babies, Mrs McKeown somehow managed to run a general store, which was all the more remarkable as she could neither read nor write.

James's father was from a strict Presbyterian background and owned no books but the Bible, which he would expound on Saturday nights in the family shop. When James was eight, a man from their church travelled down to Sunderland. He went to see a vicar who, in the wake of the great American outpouring of 1906, became the first person in the UK to minister the Baptism in the Holy Spirit. When the Glaswegian came back speaking in tongues, all the Presbyterians went to hear him but James remembers his mother begging her husband not to go anywhere near! This can have had no effect because James can still remember how horrified he felt the next day, "Mother, he's speaking in tongues! He's disgraced us!" Worse was to come a few nights later. Father looked after the family so Mother could go to the meeting and receive this strange new gift.

James said, "My father was a fine preacher but he was not good-tempered. I liked my mother better. She would laugh and sing, though she could also deliver a good smack." The children inherited their mother's dry sense of humour and all enjoyed practical jokes. Once James and a group of friends wrapped up some horse-manure, carefully making a neat parcel. They had decided to deliver it to a pompous man they knew, but somehow, when it came to the crunch, none of them dared play errand-boy – except James. He was quick. Having thrust the parcel into the man's hand he flew down the stairs and away, while his friends who had been watching were caught and given a hiding.

James's hard-working father laboured in a brick- and later, iron-works. His ambition was to buy his own farm – "and tame his wild boys in the hills of Antrim." James was eleven when his family moved to Tullynahinion near Portglenone in County Antrim. It was a long journey from Scotland with all the little ones in tow, but finally they arrived and his mother cooked eggs for tea. James sat down in the garden sunshine and fell asleep. On waking he was violently sick and never touched another egg for years.

The children soon discovered that several other large families lived nearby. There was plenty of space for them all to run and play together, and plenty of apples for the taking. It was an open landscape, with few trees. The northern wind swept over low hills and peat bogs as the farming community struggled to turn rough moorland into small green fields.

The land James's father had bought was hard and heavy. The farm had both animals and crops, but Mr McKeown had yet to learn such basics as how to build a rick or shear a sheep. James attended school for only a couple of months in Ireland before his father involved him in full-time work on the land. Soon James's young hands grew hard and bumpy with all the lifting. He spent two whole winters clearing the heather from a moorland area – a task thankless enough in itself, yet his father never gave his lad a word of encouragement. One of the younger brothers left home in disgust on hearing their father complain years later that James had failed to move a certain stone from this area.

Some light relief came from James's grandfather, who was also called James McKeown. This fierce old man had never quite forgiven James' parents for eloping and all the family were a little afraid of him – except James. Seeing this, James' grandfather would wink at his favourite grandson and slip him a special treat, or proudly announce that James had made a haystack when he had merely helped his father.

Life for the children on the farm was not all bad. As they spent much of their time in the open air, they became fascinated by the wild birds and animals. By day, larksong pulsated all around them and the "arp-arp" of the corncrake was a familiar sound as they were falling asleep. James's younger brother, Adam, later wrote, "On the farm at Tullynahinion, there is a hill, which bears two names, Mudyi and Mullinasock. To this present day that hill holds enchanted memories, not only to us little boys who herded the cows and played there, but also to the older ones, who worked and hunted there. Sometime ago I had a letter from my brother James, who, after 40 years as a Missionary in West Africa, had retired to spend his remaining years in Northern Ireland. He told me of paying a visit to Mudyi and as he sat there on its crest, surveying the countryside around, memories came flooding back, which brought tears to his eyes."[1]

Adam continues, "I well remember waking up in the early morning to the sounds which were commonplace in the farmyards of that day, but the sounds I remember most were of my mother as she busied herself with the morning chores in the big working kitchen downstairs and all the while she would be singing the hymns which were popular in that day...

1 *A Man Called Adam,* written and published by Adam McKeown.

In the years that followed, amidst all the changing experiences of life, I would hear that voice coming back to me, like some haunting refrain, and now, with hindsight, realise how much of an impact such would have on my life."

Their mother's lot was not easy – she had two more babies, Margaret and Elizabeth, at Tullynahinion – yet most of her nine children grew up to remain close to God. Of the six boys, five were later involved in Christian ministry, four of them overseas.

The family had not been long in Northern Ireland when a man who was to become arguably the greatest British evangelist of this century began his ministry there. George Jeffreys founded a group called the Elim Evangelistic Band which later became known as the Elim Four Square Gospel Alliance. They preached the Gospel of 'Christ the Saviour, Healer, Baptiser in the Holy Spirit and Coming King'. From 1915 to 1920, the Elim Band worked exclusively in Northern Ireland, starting 22 churches in the province. One of the earliest was established in a remarkable five week tent campaign which saw 120 converted and scores prostrate before the presence of God. This was in Ballymena, the McKeown's local market town and the campaign had such an effect that, when the tent was taken down, people stood weeping where it had been.

The McKeown's home became a centre of Pentecostal activity in the area and Sunday meetings at the farmhouse could continue half the night. George Jeffreys and Smith Wigglesworth were among the great Pentecostal pioneers who came to visit and minister there. To the McKeown children these great men of God were familiar figures. Even if unconsciously, they absorbed a great deal from them. James retained detailed memories of the few sermons he heard Jeffreys preach and was to put them to good use in Africa. James's and George Jeffreys' preaching styles were remarkably similar – both had a power in their preaching which did not come from noise or emotionalism.

Some of the children went through a stage when all this religion was just too much. One day, little James was in an orchard helping himself to the apples, together with his friend John Harris, whose father was also involved in the Elim revival. The guilty pair saw someone coming and ran for miles. When they found out the person was one of their young friends, and not the police, James quoted Proverbs 28:1 AV: "The wicked flee when no man pursueth." "McKeown, you're always preaching!" John accused him.

James had been brought up in a Christian home. He went to Sunday school, where his teacher thought well of him. He knew his Bible and even liked the idea of becoming a minister when he grew up. After all they got to wear special clothes and everyone knew they were very important people. But deep down, James knew he was not good. What was the use of all this religion, he thought as he grew older? He might as well enjoy himself as his friends did.

When James was nineteen, two members of the Elim Band held a campaign in his village. To James's annoyance, several of his friends were converted. Then one evening a new preacher called Robert Mercer came to John Harris' house. James later wrote, "Mr Mercer was a plain man, like myself, but there was something about him which appealed to me. I saw that he was real, and I set myself to listen to what he had to say. Lamentations 1:12 AV was his text, 'Is it nothing to you, all ye that pass by? Behold, and see if there be any sorrow like unto my sorrow.' He also read the story of the crucifixion from Mark's Gospel and I thought I had never heard it read so well. He preached on the love and suffering of Jesus Christ. I then lost sight of the preacher and this Jesus that had been so far away in my thoughts before, became very near to me. His love touched me and as I followed Jesus closely by the Word that was preached, I was full of sympathy for Him and His cause. Seeing Him led forth by cruel soldiers and set at nought by all, I felt, if I had been there, the one who took upon himself to strike Jesus would have had to strike me, for I was wholly in love with Him. The Holy Spirit making the crucifixion real to me, I was deeply moved, when, suddenly, I became aware that I was gripped by the Gospel. The tears were rolling down my cheeks but I thought I was too young to get converted – I tried to get away when the words came from the preacher, from Matthew 27:39 AV 'And they that passed by reviled Him.' "What are you going to do?" continued Mercer, "Pass Him by and take sides with those who nailed Him there or are you going to fall in love with Him and yield to His claim?"[2]

At that point, James walked out and joined his group of friends. Laughing at the hymns and choruses which filled the night air around the Harris's house, they began their own serenade. "She's the star of the County Down," yelled the lads, on their way to a late night party. When that ended they let a horse out of its stable and were back outside the Harris's kitchen window at three in the morning, making fun of the people there. Suddenly, one or two felt Mr Harris's hands on their shoulders, propelling them into the kitchen. Robert Mercer was still there. A few became Christians that night, but not James. However, back in his room, James realised that Mercer's preaching had opened his eyes to something which he could not now 'unsee' – Jesus loved him. At nineteen, James was at the age where young men do not like to be thought foolish, but, fool or not, only two more weeks went by before he stood in the meeting to announce that he belonged to Jesus.

From then on, James read his Bible regularly. "And I must say, I loved the Lord," he said, "Later on, it was that same love that took me to Africa." This falling in love with Jesus was to be the basis of James' life, the essence of all he passed on to others.

James was not the kind to make a great noise and fuss

2 Written testimonies of James and Sophia McKeown, missionaries designate to the Gold Coast, in the magazine of the Apostolic Church – *Riches of Grace,* (Convention Issue, Sept 1936)

about his new faith, but God was at work deep inside him. James had been told to seek the Baptism of the Holy Spirit but while others got the blessing, nothing happened to him. After some time he broke down and told the Lord that he had exercised all the faith he had. He said "If I don't get the blessing tonight, I'm finished." It was a strange, emptying experience, but the filling came. He felt fire come on his head and move down his body. In the end he just had to let go and ended practically throwing the bench at which he had been kneeling across the room and shouting "Glory to Jesus." Quiet as he was, he spoke with tongues "more than ye all." (I Cor 14:18 AV.)

The Holy Spirit made Jesus even more real to James and equipped him for a changed life of service. Two of the main themes of James' ministry were to be "Christ and him crucified" (I Cor 2:2 AV) and the Baptism of the Holy Spirit. Both had made a profound impression on him right at the beginning of his life as a Christian.

But James's ministry did not start very auspiciously! It was not long after his conversion that James found himself about to take an open-air evangelistic meeting. As he stood to preach for the first time in his life, he felt like a barrel with holes in it. He told the small crowd, "God has given me nothing to say, so I will sit down." The trouble was – his equally inexperienced friend did exactly the same. After the shortest meeting ever, they both fell in a ditch, howling with laughter.

James had always admired bachelors and intended never to get married. But then he saw Sophia – whom he called 'Phia', pronounced 'fire'. She was attracted to James because of his praying, she said she had never heard anyone pray like that before. "I don't know whether I can pray well or not," countered James, "but I suppose you could say it was Bible prayer." Six years older than James, Sophia also came from County Antrim. She had been educated to the advanced age of seventeen and studied dressmaking for two years, becoming a fully qualified seamstress.

Like James, Sophia came from a Presbyterian background. She became a Christian through an organisation called Faith Mission which worked in rural areas, using both men and women itinerant evangelists called Pilgrims. They stressed holiness – which was later to form the third important element in James' teaching.

One night, Sophia went to a meeting conducted by two Faith Mission Pilgrims. One of them was going out as a missionary to Africa. She laid down her life there. As the Pilgrim preached from Jesus' parable of the wise man who built his house on the rock, God spoke to Sophia. She realised that, with all her church-going, reading and praying, she was merely building upon sand – while the only sure foundation was the Rock, Jesus Christ. He was the One on whom she would pin her faith, her hopes, her all.

In 1923, Sophia fully dedicated her life in service to God, joined the Faith Mission Prayer Union, was sent out on deputation work and had hopes that she might become a Faith Mission Pilgrim. "But the Lord had still something more for me: the glorious Baptism of the Holy Ghost. There was much opposition against me going to these Holy Ghost believers, but I had caught a glimpse of 'saints on higher ground', so I was determined to scale the utmost height. I had very sweet times of fellowship with the saints in Elim."[3]

It was through Elim that Sophia first met the McKeowns – she and James were baptised by George Jeffreys in Ballymena church. In one Elim meeting around that time they were singing, "Coming, coming from afar, Afric's sons of colour deep" when a prophecy boomed out: – some from that small group would go to Africa! Years later, when James was addressing 80,000 in Accra, he thought of that prophecy. How unlikely it had seemed at the time that any of them could fulfil it – they came from such humble backgrounds!

3 *Riches of Grace.* Ibid.

James had to be able to support his wife before they could marry. There were few jobs in Northern Ireland, so he moved to Scotland to find work. He married Sophia in the summer of 1927, returning with her to Glasgow the same day. James's casual labouring work brought home little enough money, though later Sophia fulfilled a dream by opening her own dressmaking shop.

In Glasgow the McKeowns came in touch with the Apostolic Church. James discovered that they believed God was speaking to them through people they called prophets. James thought he had more sense than to believe that – sanctified common sense was his rule of guidance. But after some time, he had proof beyond doubt that God was indeed speaking to His people through the gifts He had given to His Church.

James was helped by the early Pentecostals, especially Elim, but who were these 'Apostolics'? The Apostolics split from the other Pentecostals in 1916, and from then on, had little to do with other Christians. Their headquarters remains in the tiny South Wales village of Penygroes, which was originally home to their leader, Dan Powell Williams and his brother, William Jones Williams. Unlike the other Pentecostals, they believed prophecy should give specific direction to the church. Through prophecy men were chosen to be apostles, prophets, evangelists, pastors and teachers. There were also offices of elder and deacon in the local assembly.

At first the Apostolics saw phenomenal growth and many moves of God. They were keen on missionary work from the beginning – in fact the denomination flourished overseas far more than it did in the UK. Today there are less than 170 British assemblies, as against 3,000 in Nigeria.

In 1919 an independent Pentecostal group in Glasgow affiliated with the Apostolics. Andrew Turnbull, a ploughman-turned-evangelist, led this group. It became known as 'The Burning Bush' because Turnbull used to say,

"Get on fire for God and men will come to see you burn." Miraculous healing and exorcisms were common. Many were saved and new churches sprang up right across Scotland.

In 1930, Andrew Turnbull visited Nigeria with the Williams brothers. Turnbull had always wanted to preach the Gospel to Africans. For some reason he felt a special love for them. Was it co-incidence that this was the very man in charge of the church where James and Sophia became involved?

Even before James became a member of the Apostolic church in Glasgow, someone prophesied that he should be the elder presiding over that assembly. The other elders disagreed and James kept quiet – he did not want to be an elder. However, he stuck with the group, because he did like going to the open-air evangelistic meetings and giving his testimony. Soon James was not only made an elder but was 'put on the plan'. This meant he was sent to preach at assemblies and conventions all over Scotland. Sophia was made a deaconess. In 1933, James invited his brother Adam to the Apostolic annual new year convention. "It was like heaven on earth," Adam wrote, "There were violins, mandolins, organ, piano, tambourines and dancing before the Lord." However, James was uneasy about some things in the Apostolic church. As he grew closer to the inner circle, he came to believe that some so-called directive prophecies were manufactured to fit in with decisions which men had already made.

Work was short and notices went up advertising that the Canadians wanted thousands of workers for their harvest. James applied. He was asked, "Are you going out married or single?" James had never told a lie and just managed to avoid doing so now by saying, "I'm going out single, Sir!" They told him the next day's boat was full. There were, however, a few spaces on a boat leaving that afternoon. Hurrying home, James just had time for a cup of tea while Sophia packed his things and then he was off on his first trip abroad. The Apostolics suspended James from membership for six months because he disappeared without a word to them.

His first Sunday in Canada, James went along to a church service. As he was chatting afterwards, the minister approached him and asked him to preach. "How do you know I'm a runaway from the Apostolics?" demanded James. The minister was so impressed with the sermon that he asked James to take over his church for a few months while he made a trip down south. He was even prepared to pay Sophia's fare to Canada. James liked the idea but when he prayed about it, God said "No." "Then I was sorry I prayed!" said James – but he knew the most important thing was to hear and obey God's voice. No matter how much he would have liked to stay, James came straight back after the harvest. Physically stronger than ever from the hard work in Canada, he returned to his labouring jobs. Sophia fumed about the missed opportunity, but at least the Apostolics were so anxious for James to preach again, that he heard no more about the six months suspension.

James wrote, "The Word of God through prophecy called me forth, step by step, to public ministry, which was very severe on my reserved make-up, but grace was given to follow Him who was calling. My experience taught me not to be exercised about ambitious desires, but to love the Lord and shine where I was placed. Having this settled in my heart, peace reigned, and while I admired others who went forth to other lands, I never dreamed that such was for me. 'What matters where on earth we dwell?' It's Jesus that matters."[4]

Soon the work situation improved. An inspector on Glasgow's trams put James's name forward to be a trams conductor, a job which James enjoyed, because it involved contact with people. Even in those days, black men rode on his tram. James was always very interested in them and

4 *Riches of Grace.* Ibid.

thought how lovely they were. Later he came to drive the tram and earned a living wage at last.

## Gold Coast calling

If God was working in James's life over these years, He was working in the Gold Coast too. But there was something missing, you might say a James-shaped-hole had developed in the ministry out there. Since the 1840s, various Christian missions had done good work, especially the Methodists and Presbyterians. Increasingly, however, they put social concerns, such as schools and trading, above evangelism. Though the elite of the country responded to this approach, the ordinary man tended to dismiss Christianity as the religion of white people and of the ruling class.

Most missions produced little models of their own church back home. The Methodists have always been recognisable as English Methodists; the same principle applies to others such as the Salvation Army, and the Presbyterian Basel and Bremen Missions. Often, the new Christians lived apart from the rest of the town and wore European dress. Most Africans found this sort of Christianity irrelevant, but they still had spiritual needs. Sadly, this meant all sorts of strange cults flourished, often quasi-Christian cults where the Bible was not read, just waved about like some magical talisman to ward off evil spirits.

In 1917, a magazine called *Sword of the Spirit* found its way to the Gold Coast from the Faith Tabernacle Church in Philadelphia. Its main preoccupation was with healing, but through it, an African called Peter Anim realised that faith involved more than the intellectual agreement he had reached with the Presbyterians. Anim became a Christian, was healed of long-standing stomach trouble and moved to an inland town in Eastern Region called Asamankese. There his preaching gained a group of converts; many were healed and this attracted others. In 1926, Anim read about the Holy

Spirit in another magazine, this time from the Apostolic Faith in America. He wanted to know more, but the Faith Tabernacle did not approve and he was expelled from any association with them. Anim discovered that the leader of Faith Tabernacle in Nigeria had travelled a similar path, and had invited three British Apostolics to visit Nigeria. These were none other than James's Glasgow pastor – Andrew Turnbull – and the Williams brothers. They landed in Accra. Anim and two others met them off the ship and accompanied them on their visit to Nigeria.

When Anim returned to the Gold Coast, all his people longed to be filled with the Spirit. As it happened, the first Ghanaian Christian to experience this was a Presbyterian from Akim Akroso, 12 miles to the south of Asamankese. James Gyimah was considered a lunatic by his church, but he began preaching and speaking in tongues on the streets of Akroso, to large crowds attracted by the phenomenon. Eventually, he won over most of the leading members in his Presbyterian church. These included S R Asomaning and J A Bimpon – who, with Gyimah himself, were to become three of James' earliest pastors. Akroso became a lively assembly in fellowship with Anim's. The next year the Spirit came upon the Asamankese believers and a revival spread out from the town.

In 1935, a visiting Apostolic pastor so impressed Anim's groups in Asamankese that they became affiliated to his denomination, taking the name "Apostolic Church, Gold Coast." The following year, another Bradford Apostolic recommended they have a permanent missionary, and Anim asked only that this be delayed for a year so they could find suitable accommodation for him.

It seemed as though Anim would be disappointed because, back in England, the Apostolics had no money to send out more missionaries at that time. But a little later, at a large Apostolic convention in England, someone prophesied that James and Sophia McKeown should go as missionaries to West Africa. This seemed strange in view of the leadership decision to send no-one, and even stranger because James and Sophia were not even at the convention, but far away in Glasgow. Strangest of all, nothing was said to them, though vague rumours began to percolate through after several weeks.

Finally, James was visited by the Executive of the church, who told him about the prophecy. For a moment James thought back to all the missionary books he had loved to read as a boy. But it was astounding that they should ask *him* to go on the mission field! “Friends,” James said, “you know I left school at the age of eleven. I really think missionaries need more education than I have received!” The leaders replied that James had something many educated people did not have and that was adaptability. “I thank you,” said James, “but still I feel strongly that my training is inadequate for such a job. I will not agree to go with my wife as a missionary.”

Having refused the call, 15 months went by until James awoke in the night to hear his wife crying. “Whatever is the matter?” he asked. Sophia was pleading that they go as missionaries. “What can you do when your wife is crying at your back every night?” asked James. “I agreed to go and gave up my job as a tram driver in Glasgow.” James wrote, shortly before he left England, “The call then came forth that it was the will of God for my wife and me to be planted in the soil of Africa. Like all other experiences with the Lord, it seemed strange at first, but after inquiring in the secret of His Presence, the call has become the sole passion of my life.”[5] His aunt did not see it that way. She commented, “Are you the only soft nob they have to go to Africa?”.

James was supplied with clerical collars. Insecure as ever about his education, as he prepared to leave, James made sure these were sent ahead in his suitcases to Liverpool docks. “It was all very well wearing a clerical collar, but as soon as I opened my mouth, I broke all the rules of English

5 *Riches of Grace.* Ibid.

grammar!" lamented James, "though I must admit, when some village Chiefs in Africa saw my round collar, they showed great respect. Some thought I was a University graduate!" James left on the boat in February 1937, but as he did not know what to expect in Africa, he asked Sophia to stay in the UK for a few months.

# Chapter 3

# Signs, Wonders and a Split.

James headed for Africa with Scofield Bible, sun-hat and little idea of what to expect. Sophia, waving her husband off on the quayside, had to be content with promises that he would write. Fifty years make a big difference in travel terms – today, once you have gone through the lengthy programme of injections and obtaining a visa, a jet takes just six hours to cover the 3,000 miles due south to Accra. In 1937 the journey to the British Gold Coast took eleven days by steamer. James had never heard of inoculations and the man-made harbour was yet to be built.

On the 4th of March, 1937, the steamer anchored off Accra. Huge, Atlantic waves pounded over the bar. Surf boats made of hollowed-out tree trunks were the only means by which passengers and cargo could reach dry land. It was not as dangerous as it looked – the fishermen who handled the boats were very skilled – but they took delight in bumping passengers down into their primitive craft before the hair-raising ride in to shore on the surf.

Anim had sent a couple of Africans to meet James on the beach and they took him straight to Asamankese by car – a hot, bumpy journey fifty-six miles up-country. Leaving the sprawling capital city behind, they crossed the scrubland of the coastal plain, passing through villages which seemed to specialise: one for example baking bread, another growing pineapples. When they had to slow down, dark-skinned children clustered around, waving and grinning. All along the roadside women walked, graceful despite their huge head loads and the babies tied on their backs.

Soon the car was travelling through tropical rain forest where the great, flanged tree roots were like nothing James had ever seen before. It was only when he looked up at the height of the straight grey tree trunks, with their long branches, covered in bromeliads, that James realised why such flying-buttress roots were necessary.

The heat really hit James once he arrived in Asamankese. In a moving car or boat at least there was some breeze, but here the clothes stuck to his skin. James discovered that the church had not finished the house they were building for him and that for some reason he was lodged with a pagan man who had three wives and twenty-six children. "I can picture that compound today," he said, with a shudder. "I'd no sooner met my new landlord than he asked me to pray that God would give him yet more children!"

James changed the subject and, fanning himself with a piece of paper, asked, "Is it always this hot?" "At night it is quite chilly sometimes," replied his landlord, but when James asked if he ever needed a blanket, the man looked horrified at the thought. All James wanted was a drink and after he had downed what felt like pints of water, he felt better. "Don't spill a drop!" warned his landlord, "Or we'll have the ants in." Left alone, James could hear the sound of wood being chopped nearby and from every compound came a dull, regular 'thump, thump, thump'. The women were pounding yam, cassava and plantain ready for their evening meal of their staple food, *fu-fu.*

Darkness fell suddenly at six and James experienced his first African night. It was slightly cooler than the day, so the air was able to hold less moisture, and felt unbearably humid. Drums started up just down the road, together with what sounded like drunken singing, but by nine-thirty, all the people seemed to have gone to bed. James retired too, but it was far from quiet. The ceaseless chorous of cicadas and frogs, and the unidentified howls emphasised just how far he was from home. Today, TV images prepare us for Africa but it still comes as a culture shock: James must have found the change of environment extraordinary.

At four the next morning, though it was still pitch dark,

James was startled by ear-piercing cock-crows, coming from near and far. Before long the whole town seemed up and busy. There were more thumpings and grindings. In the street outside James's window passers-by were chanting and singing. As soon as day-light allowed, James washed and dressed and by six-thirty had ventured outside. He was surprised to find the sun already so high in the sky it was evaporating pools of dew on the dripping plants.

People grinned and said "hello" or "bye-bye" – maybe the only English words they knew. Many of the men carried large machetes. One spoke good English and James asked what he was doing. "I'm going to farm, and I will use my knife to plough," he replied. James thought of the horse-drawn ploughs of Ireland and felt homesick, but a least a farm sounded familiar and he headed out of town in search of one. After some time he thought, "If all these men with machetes are really going to their farms, why can't I find any?" It was only later that he discovered that tropical crops are scattered in the bush and look nothing like the farms back home. An African 'ploughed field' describes an area where machetes have slashed the forest vegetation. On the other hand, James found plenty that was exotic – orange and green lizards, rust-coloured anthills as tall as himself and tiny scarlet birds. Butterflies, huge and yellow, fluttered amidst dark greenery which grew like office pot-plants gone mad. Great creepers wound up the trees. Cocoa pods and bananas hung ripening in the sun.

By now it was eight o'clock and, wishing he had brought a hat, James headed back towards his lodgings. Vultures dominated the skies and even perched on the town's roof tops. It was time for yet more water and another bath. This was the hottest time of year and James really knew he was in Africa.

The small town of Asamankese was a remote spot and James was the only white person living among five thousand Africans. Despite the fact that all of them seemed to want to come and greet the new *obruni* (white man) with much hand-shaking and formal ceremony, as time went by James felt out of place and very lonely, only wishing Sophia were with him. There were two things he longed to see – a post office and the Throne of Grace!

The post was erratic, though some letters must have got through because Sophia complained his were not detailed enough. So he described the state of dress of the women who pounded their cassava below his balcony. That was quite graphic enough for Sophia, who replied, "Your letter is disgraceful!" More seriously, money often failed to reach James from home and the local church had not yet learnt to tithe, so finances were lean.

Despite all these difficulties, James was not one to sit around feeling sorry for himself – there was plenty to do. He had come to plant seeds, his brief being no less than to help establish the Apostolic Church in the Gold Coast and to preach the Gospel to the pagan peoples there. James wrote about the difficulties of adapting to the rhythm of life in this new country. "At twelve noon the sun is high in the heavens and it is very hot. One feels the nature of the day changing. Heaviness comes down upon all. There are no cocks crowing now, no sheep or goats running about, they have all taken to the shade. The villager spreads out his mat in the shade and sinks down in slumber. The energetic European would like to carry on. There is a language to be learnt, there is a call from home for reports and there is preparation to be made for the services. But in spite of the desire to go on, the mind is not active, the writing and spelling get bad, and one learns that it is better to obey nature's voice and to take a rest."[1]

Soon after James arrived, Anim gathered all his people at a service in Asamankese, to welcome their new missionary. James was impressed with their singing, 'We'll storm the force of darkness, bring them down.' Their welcome was

1 Pastor J McKeown, "Life in an African Village", *The Herald of Grace*, (July 1941): p 101.

warm and James in his turn won the Africans' hearts by mixing freely with them and refusing to stand on ceremony. He even helped them build the mission house with his own hands and, despite the sticky heat, walked up to 40 miles through the bush to outlying groups. In those days of colonialism the Africans were amazed that a white man lived as they lived, and did not mind in what primitive conditions he slept. Since there was not a turnip or potato in sight, James ate the local food: the gritty cassava, the ground-nut stew which tastes like curried peanut-butter, and fu-fu, a kind of dough which must be swallowed whole because it sticks to the teeth if chewed. James thought some people could make very good fu-fu. Other Ghanaian delicacies range through maggots and giant snails, to a kind of large rat. James grew used to dredging his food with salt, to supplement body-salts lost through perspiration. Not only that – Ghanaian food is cooked with so many spices, it can make Indian curry seem tame. Still, James made a habit of eating whatever was put before him, "But I liked pineapples best," he said.

On one level, all was going well, but James was worried. In West Africa, all sorts of diseases are rife, and, not surprisingly, native churches often emphasise the healing aspects of the Gospel. Africans are drawn to the supernatural, but problems occur when healing becomes more important to them than salvation. Anim's people believed Christians should look only to Jesus for healing; a doctor was the Devil. Anyone who took medicine would go to hell and was subject to the same church discipline as if they had been involved in sexual immorality or demon worship. Sores were not dressed. Wearing glasses was a sin – they said it was worshipping the god of sand (glass being made of sand.) If someone broke his leg, splints were outlawed and prayer the only remedy. Women in childbirth were told that their faith was sufficient – they should allow no one to assist them. Sadly, many mothers and babies died.

James was in a difficult position. He did not share this extreme view on faith healing, believing Jesus could save whether or not a person took medicine. Nowhere in James's Bible did it say taking medicine was sin. Night after night James cried himself to sleep as he heard of Africans dying for the lack of simple and available medical care. He also realised that if the British government associated him, as a white missionary, with such dangerous beliefs, he would be in trouble. Anim and his followers held this no-medication doctrine as the most important part of their faith, so when they realised their missionary did not agree, they became even more insistent about it. To make matters worse, James found some of the church leaders telling lies, especially about money. Soon, though James was a quiet man, he found he had made many enemies. It was as though the seed he had come to establish had some genetic fault in it from the beginning.

One day, James took stock and realised that all his crying was not doing any good. His Irish sense of humour took over. At the next meeting he preached about Caleb, who at 85 was fit and strong, because he wholly followed the Lord. He asked the congregation, "Do you believe that, if you wholly follow the Lord, *you* won't need a stick or glasses at 85?" At last the people thought, "Our missionary – he preach divine healing proper." James went to bed happy and there was no crying that night.

Next meeting he preached about Moses at 120, "His eyes were not weak nor his strength gone, because he wholly followed the Lord. Do you Africans believe that if you do the same you will not need glasses?" At this, what James had been waiting for happened – the senior pastor, who did wear spectacles, surreptitiously slipped them into his pocket!

This incident appealed to James's dry sense of humour, but he had been in the country only three months when the inevitable happened. He would trek through the bush and hold meetings in the open at night but took no quinine or any special precautions. He went down with malaria so badly he thought it was the end, and prepared to die, mentally saying farewell to his wife and family. Taking a last look out of the window, James saw a flame tree, whose blossom was so red it startled him. "If there is so much beauty in the world, how can I die?" he thought. Then he dreamt he was struggling with blackness, until, suddenly a great light dispersed it and he shouted, "Hallelujah!" This was a kind of turning-point, but his fever was still high.

The District Commissioner, on trek, heard how ill James had become and arranged for him to be sent to hospital. The nearest one was closed, so James was taken, semi-conscious, all the way to Accra. Realising this would be an horrendous journey, but not appreciating that James was teetotal, the DC instructed the boy accompanying James to give him whisky. When they finally arrived, the bottle was empty! After all this, when James finally regained consciousness in the European hospital, he thought the white nurse who looked after him was "like an angel".

James responded to treatment and was discharged after eleven days. He went straight back to continue his work in Asamankese, but the church felt betrayed that their missionary had gone so far against their teaching as to receive hospital treatment. They enjoyed his preaching, but felt he had no faith. James found they no longer trusted him. He took lemon juice and they accused him of using medicine. Worse, he was discouraged from preaching the Gospel in outlying villages where they could not keep an eye on him.

Sophia arrived in the September. With typical understatement, James said, "I was glad to see her." Determined to join her husband despite a doctor's warnings that she was too frail to stand the African sun, Sophia had travelled with a Pastor Taylor who was bound for the Apostolic's larger mission field in Nigeria. Just before these two left, someone had an 'encouraging' prophecy – one of them would be dead within the year! Everyone assumed this would be Sophia and not the large, strong pastor. Undeterred, Sophia said God knew James had a wife and had called them both to do missionary work in Africa. In fact, Sophia was seldom unwell all her years in Ghana but by July 1938, poor Pastor Taylor had died of dysentery in Nigeria. "Did you notice anything about his eating habits on the ship?" James asked Sophia. When she said she noticed him lick the sauce bottle, James said, "There you are – hygiene is important in Africa!"

As the only white woman in Asamankese, Sophia was held in high regard. The elders would not allow her to preach, but she passed on her skills in cookery and needlework to the women and girls of the town. At one stage, Sophia was alone for several weeks in Asamankese as James had gone to help a newly established church in Winneba, a coastal town some 40 miles away.

Then, about a year after his hospitalisation, matters came to a head in Asamankese. There was such a lack of trust that James was hindered from doing the work for which he had come. He asked for a change of station – to Winneba, where he would be more free to evangelise and plant churches. The Asamankese elders were reluctant, though others, especially those in Akroso, saw the wisdom of James's stance on healing. In June 1938, James and Sophia, with two native house-girls, set off for Winneba. They had no money, until a postal order for ten pounds arrived unexpectedly from Britain. The final break with Asamankese did not come until June 1939, but they had little to do with Anim after this. The McKeowns were effectively starting by themselves from scratch.

Later, many of the people from Anim's outlying groups joined James and several Akroso men were among his earliest pastors. The Apostolic missionary headquarters at Bradford did not agree with the no-medication doctrine, so Anim split from them and renamed his church 'Christ Apostolic.' This still exists in Ghana, but is comparatively small – for example, figures in 1986 for Ghana's Eastern

Region, which includes Asamankese, shows the Christ Apostolic with 6,642 attending church, compared to the Church of Pentecost's 44,973.

## Healing

This part of Africa used to be known as 'The White Man's Grave' – and not without reason. The missionaries who bravely queued up to go to the Gold Coast from 1838 onwards survived an average of six months. All the tropical diseases are common – yellow fever, bilharzia, cholera, typhoid.... the list goes on. Uncooked food must be sterilised, water too, even if it is only used for brushing teeth. Hanging clothes outside to dry is hazardous – parasites might lay eggs on them which later hatch and burrow into the skin. So apart from Sophia taking sensible precautions, how was it the McKeowns had so few health problems while they were in Ghana? It is ironic that James split from Anim defending the possibility of taking medicine and then needed to use very little himself.

James trusted God, believing that if He is in charge, these things are His responsibility, not ours. In addition, James came to realise that states of anxiousness affect our health more than we know. Friends said the McKeowns had that constant sense of peace which comes from a close walk with God. Apart from very minor ailments, James was ill in Ghana only twice after his malaria attack – both times he had lost that peace. The first happened a few days after all his possessions were stolen. Sophia had hysterics, but James remained calm at the time: his feelings came out later in delayed shock and illness. The second occasion was after James lost his temper with another missionary. The man had been provoking him for some time, but God had spoken very specifically to James that he should not rise to the bait. Disobedience freed emotions which gave rise to an ulcer that troubled him for years.

Recently, church growth in many parts of the world has been linked with healing, signs and wonders. Throughout the Church of Pentecost's history there are reports of remarkable miracles, but everywhere there seemed a strange reluctance to talk about the subject. One of the apostles explained. James taught that it was more important to have your name written in the Lamb's Book of Life than to experience signs and wonders. James had learnt his lesson from Asamankese. Man has a natural tendency, especially in Africa, to put signs and wonders before his relationship with Jesus. If some of the miracles the Church saw in Ghana had occurred in America they would have been promoted as front page news. Many have pandered to the sensational: James always played it down and he paid the price with obscurity.

After close questioning, James went so far as to say that he asked God to show him the state of heart of those who would be at outreach meetings. If God said they needed signs to confirm the word he preached, James prayed for the sick and they were healed – but the Ghanaians pointed out the greatest miracles in his ministry were the changed lives. "If someone is healed he can go off and later become a drunkard, but if someone preaches and your life is changed – it is a miracle."

With all the sickness and infant mortality, ordinary people were certainly attracted to any who offered healing. The witch-doctors claimed cures, so did the many African cults which combined elements of the old religion with Christianity. The mainstream churches, on the other hand, failed to proclaim that Christ heals today.

All sorts of extremes have been associated with healing in Ghana, but that does not mean Jesus cannot heal. James encouraged his people to reach their full potential in Jesus and many saw far more miracles than James did himself. The Gospel had never been heard in many remote areas before James sent out evangelists. People believed in witchcraft and prayed to fetish gods which were very powerful. The only way in which they would believe in Jesus was if it were demonstrated that He was more powerful than their gods – so the evangelists prayed for signs and miracles. They saw the lame walk, the blind see, even the dead raised. Large numbers of people realised that this was more than the form of words of some irrelevant white man's religion: they saw Jesus was real and turned to Him in large numbers. The same is true today. The town of Tamale in the north of Ghana is 80% Moslem and the Gospel has made little headway there, but recently some spectacular miracles in a Reinhard Bonnke crusade drew 50,000 to a single meeting. Even the Moslems were saying, "The hallelujah God is powerful!" and some joined the Church.

Even though the Church never looked for publicity from healings, when a life-long cripple runs home to his village, it is bound to have an effect. Whole assemblies have been opened as a result of such miracles. People take notice. For example, a midwife, working in a strongly fetish area noticed that women who had the mark of the fetish on them had trouble delivering, whereas the Apostolics had straightforward births. One day, she examined an Apostolic lady and found medical reasons why she would only be able to give birth by Caesarian section. The Church asked if they could pray before their member was sent to hospital and when she gave birth quite normally, the midwife began asking them about Jesus. This midwife now leads the Church of Pentecost's Women's Movement in Greater Accra.

There are healing ministries operating within the Church, though James' caution was borne out by the fact that many of the men who had this ministry in the past have objected to coming under the discipline of the Church as a whole and have split away to found their own works. Nevertheless, today the Church finds many new converts through three 'Prayer and Healing Camps' run by women with healing ministries. Barrenness is the greatest disgrace a Ghanaian woman can face. Many have resorted to magic, but God has provided an answer in that the camps seem particularly sucessful in praying for childless women. But all sorts of other people, from top government officials down, have been to a prayer meeting at one of these camps or stayed there to fast and pray for a longer period. People come to the camps from all over West Africa and not only are many healed, but hundreds find Jesus for themselves and are directed to their local pastor back home for follow up and baptism.

Many of us are insulated from the world. We wonder why we see few miracles, why our level of faith is so low. Someone said, "We have not lost faith – we have simply transferred it to the medical profession." In the USA there is one doctor for every 500 people. In Ghana, he would be shared among 75,000. If Church members themselves fall ill there is often little medical help available. They have no alternative but to look to God, though he does not always answer in the way they expect. David Mills once developed a rash on his neck, caused by the dust from the wings of a certain moth. Every time the blisters burst, the painful infection spread further and the doctor uttered those familiar words, "Nothing I can do – take some aspirin." One of James's old pioneer apostles said he would bring something for it and returned with a pot of vile, greenish mud. "Spread this on your neck with a stick," he said, "and in three days, when it is dry, crack it off and your skin will be as good as new." David was sceptical about native medicine, but it happened as the apostle said. Apparently, some years before, a young boy in his church had this rash spread all over his body. The mother was desperate and the church fasted and prayed. God spoke to them and told them which leaves to gather to make the paste. Not only was the boy healed, but, said the apostle, it is a sure-fire cure every time.

When we were in Ghana, the Good Friday sermon dealt with all that had been accomplished through Jesus' sufferings and death. Afterwards, those who were sick were called forward and hundreds squeezed in front of the platform to stand in the hot sun. The thousands of us who remained extended our hands towards them and prayed out loud – an awesome sound. After a few minutes, a song-leader began singing from the platform, but the prayer continued unabated. Later, there was time for only a fraction of the queue of people who wanted to tell how Jesus had just healed them, but some who did reach the microphone were excitedly moving parts of themselves they had not moved for years.

In Ghana, whether in healing or other areas, people's faith and expectancy that God will move matches the results they see, but it has not always been easy. When James and Sophia left Asamankese to start work all over again, they must have felt their faith in the God Who had called them was being tested as never before.

# Chapter 4
# "Where Two or Three..."

With an uncertain future and £10 in hand, James and Phia moved to Winneba. This small coastal town, 40 miles south of Asamankese, was a pleasant place to live. A cooling breeze blew off the sea and fresh fish was always available.

In many ways, James must have felt, 15 months into his first missionary term in the Gold Coast, that he was starting again from scratch. In fact, James did have some contacts. When Anim's people had begun work in the town, James himself had walked all the way from Asamankese in order to hold some rallies in Winneba. On the first night alone, just before Christmas 1937, 60 people had become Christians. James had stayed for some weeks in Winneba with a young man called J. Cofie Quaye, who was later to become very significant in the Church. In addition, many in Akroso maintained links with James. Others in the area, associating the McKeowns with the 'no-medication' church, would have nothing to do with them.

James and Sophia rented part of a well-built house and from here would walk quite a distance to preach in Winneba's market place. One evening, just after they had moved in, James was praying in his room and thought he heard a voice saying, "Let your house boy stay and keep watch at the house while you preach in the market place tonight." The boy, however, was so keen to go to the meeting, James did not have the heart to stop him. Again in the meeting the voice seemed to be saying "send him home". As James hurried back, he was met by the Dutch Catholic Father who lived in the other half of their house. He had been in his chapel when he also felt he must get home. Hearing noises coming from James' part of the house, he realised there were burglars and gave chase, whereupon the men dropped some of the boxes they had been carrying, and escaped.

When James returned to the house, it was in a real mess. All their things had been taken and Sophia became hysterical. The next day God told James where the thieves had dropped most of their loot in the bush and he was able to retrieve it. A few weeks later, the Catholic priest's vestments disappeared, and again, God told James where to find them.

James hired a hall for Sunday services and Sunday School. He also started evangelising the countryside and nearby towns, but, in one sense, the Church really began when a well-educated woman by the name of Mrs Christiana Obo came to one of a series of meetings James held at Saltpond (a small town just along the coast from Winneba.) Mrs Obo was a UTC agent, which meant she was entitled to collect goods from this powerful trading company and sell them again, so she was quite wealthy. The day before the meetings were to end, Mrs Obo came across an invitation to them and thought, "This is my last opportunity, I will go." Sitting at the very back, she was impressed by a tall young man called McKeown, whose preaching seemed different from anything she had heard before.

Next morning, in order to be able to come to the final meeting, Mrs Obo closed her stall. Arriving early, she sat at the front, where James noticed her. He would often sense God was working in a special way in certain individuals, even when he did not know them. As he preached on the call of Matthew, Mrs Obo just beamed and something in her encouraged James in his preaching. As she continued to look intently at his face, James knew Jesus had touched her.

Mrs Obo went up to James afterwards. "You have what I want!" she said. "Tell me, is this Holy Ghost real? Is it all true today? Can we be Baptised in the Holy Spirit?" James said "You have your Bible," and took her through the Scriptures until she was convinced.

Mrs Obo was a leader in the Methodist Church. The

Methodist pastor could not understand why she wanted to leave, but Mrs Obo said, "You and I attended that man's rally – did you hear what he said? The Holy Ghost is for us too!" The minister could not see the problem since they believed the same in the Methodist Church. "Well," said Mrs Obo, "I have been a Methodist a long time and you are my pastor, but you have never spoken like this about the Holy Spirit. If this man had not preached it in the open air, how would we know? I am leaving!"

Mrs Obo had a daughter called Eunice. At the time, she was seventeen years old and at school in Cape Coast. When her mother wrote to say she had left the respectable Methodist Church with its fine buildings to meet with this small group, Eunice was worried and longed for the end of term so she could come home and see what was wrong. Back in Saltpond, Eunice found a handful of people meeting in someone's dilapidated shed. It was lit by one lantern and had a cheap carpenter's table, without even a cloth on it. Eunice thought her mother had gone mad and sat waiting for them to pray so she could laugh – she had imagined they would be like children praying. But when one of the girls started prophesying, the word went straight into Eunice like a dart. She gave her heart to Jesus that very evening, amazed to find herself speaking in tongues straightaway, even before her mother.

*Obo* means 'rock' and Mrs Obo became a real rock in the foundation of the Church. Wealthy women in the Gold Coast wore their gold ear-rings and other ornaments with pride. Mrs Obo gave all hers to James, so he could sell them to finance the penniless Church. She also organised the women at Saltpond for Bible study and later taught women all over Ghana how to pray and evangelise. She led the Women's Movement in the Church from its inception in 1938 until 1974. It was with women that the Church began. The problem was that there were few men who were prepared to lead.

Mrs Obo's husband had left her and remarried in England. James often stayed in remote bush villages and felt some places were too primitive for Sophia. Mrs Obo travelled with him as translator, but she saw there was a problem – people might get the wrong impression if they were seen so often together. She determined to do something about it.

There was a Methodist schoolmaster in Abura Dunkwa by the name of Morrison. He and his family had been baptised in the Holy Spirit and he was coming to join James, but the Methodists would not allow it. Mrs Obo took it upon herself to go to Abura Dunkwa and beg someone to come and interpret for James. Mrs Obo had heard of J. A. C. Anaman, who had Methodist connections. When she promised that whatever she earned from her store-keeping should go to help provide for him, Anaman consented to come. He was a clever and witty man and an excellent interpreter.

By June, 1939, total numbers in James's Church had reached about 200. James held his first ever convention, drawing all the groups together in Winneba. There the first Africans were called to be elders. As James laid his hands on Anaman, to ordain him overseer to Saltpond, he found himself beginning to prophesy, "This man will both deceive and betray you." Though he pulled himself together and straightened his words, his prayer was still very confused. Three weeks later the man did betray him, but came back "with crying eyes", saying he would never do it again. Later years were to prove the accuracy of the prophecy and Anaman was the source of many of James's troubles. Mrs Obo and the women could also see what sort of a man Anaman was, but because there were few men willing to serve, they undertook to pray for him one whole morning every week. They saw him change and become used of God for many years until he attempted to oust James in 1960.

The other man James laid hands on was the first pastor of the Church, S. R. Asomaning, from Akroso. He was a very faithful pastor. Also, a man named R. O. Hayford was ordained as an evangelist at this time. By the end of 1940 they had another pastor called D. K. Boateng – all three had formerly been with Anim.

The McKeown's first furlough started just after the convention in June, 1939. This was to be the last time they saw the UK for a number of years. The normal schedule was two and a half years on the field and six month's furlough, but the war interrupted that. When they returned to the Gold Coast their boat was in a convoy escorted by the navy, because many passenger boats on this route were sunk.

Numerical growth of the Church in Ghana was far from spectacular at this stage, yet the years James spent in Winneba were some of the most significant, because the Church learnt to pray. "Not that it was hard to get Africans to pray!" James explained. "Numbers might have been small, but where two or three are gathered in the name of Jesus, His presence can change everything."

James was only too conscious that, on his own, he was finite. But God had sent him to build this Church and God is infinite. James knew that if the Church was to become great, it would be through prayer. He began to teach the little band of people about the benefits of being at one with God through prayer. He made it clear that, although neither he nor they were anything special, God could speak to them through revelations and visions.

Much later, when the Church had grown large, James' main burden, even in business meetings, was that people should pray. For example, in 1973 James said that the Church of Pentecost was growing numerically and financially but if the secret place of waiting on God was neglected the Church would decline, and decay set in. He continued, "At the commencement of the work, 40 years ago, there was prayer and yet more prayer. If we follow education, we will get what education gives. If we follow material things, we will get what they give. We have to seek the Lord and wait on Him – this is the secret of the Church's success and expansion."

If asked, James said he based his prayer life on Hebrews chapter 10 – the new and living way that Jesus' blood has opened up for us to the Father. "Prayer is worship first," he would say, "being in an attitude of prayer, not just asking – it's a two-way communication. Then sometimes, I just remember people."

James once wrote, "We should always act in tune with the sweet voice of God – which should be as familiar as the voice of the shepherd to his sheep. After all the worries of the day we should lose the ego of "I" and go to sleep so that God can communicate with our hearts. By loving Jesus and our fellow men we bring complete healing to our minds and bodies..... While waiting to hear the loving voice of our Lord we should let go the worries and cares of this world which make a noise in our hearts and hinder the Lord from communicating with us."

In the end, it was not so much a matter of teaching the people how to pray – more that they caught James' own passion for prayer. The Africans found that James would rather pray than preach, or go to many meetings. When they visited his home they would usually find James in the corner, quietly praying. They noticed he went to bed early and he explained this was so that he could rise early and pray. They began to realise the secret of his strength was that he had learnt to pray without ceasing.

The tiny Church spent much of their early meetings in prayer and there were many prophecies. Mrs Obo opened her house to women who came and prayed from four or five till ten in the morning. They continued this practice over a long period of time – just crying to God to lift up his hand and bring people to know Christ.

Mrs Obo and a lady called Prudence Anaman also spent days in the bush, weeping. They did not know how to pray, but they cried to God, "The people won't come. This lovely Jesus has been lifted up and they are not attracted." They wept and wept and wept. Then, one day Pastor Asomaning stood up to prophesy and said he saw a man sitting on a white horse, trotting, trotting all over Ghana. He held a sceptre in his hand. There were then just two or three small assemblies; they wondered – how could this great prophecy come to pass?

It was slow and difficult at the start, but eventually God really came down, not just in word but with signs and wonders – to the extent that many were in awe of this small group of ordinary Africans who prayed. Sinners came in weeping, confessing their sins. No-one had told them anything, but the presence of God was there to change their lives. The Holy Spirit caused people to confess things they had managed to hide for years. There were some miraculous conversions. Other people said the group was anti-Christ, declaring, for example, that there was fasting because the people involved were poor and did not have enough to eat anyway.

The Church had no facilities of their own – they had to hire buildings for evangelistic meetings – so, whenever possible, people would get together and go off into the bush to pray. Some went as many as three times a day.

Bush prayer meetings were never dull – often people would be healed or delivered. This in turn drew many people who came to know Jesus. In the late 1940s, Adam McKeown came to help his brother in the Church. Adam writes, "We had gone into the bush for our usual morning prayer meeting where quite a company, mainly women, were gathered, seeking God. After a word of exhortation we commenced to pray, and while encouraging those who were seeking for the baptism in the Holy Spirit, one young woman was tossed down and thrown about in a wild manner until her face and clothing were covered with red earth. We continued to pray and claim deliverance in the name of Jesus, until her struggles ceased and she laid quiet. We listened to the young woman's testimony later, how that for years she had been troubled by epileptic fits and was gradually getting worse. She believed in the prayer meeting in the bush and had been gloriously delivered and healed."[1]

James said he loved to pray under the shade of those huge trees, even though at times he resorted to Wellington boots as protection against unwelcome wildlife.

Adam continues, "These meetings in the bush are a real source of blessing and are greatly enjoyed by all concerned. One of our Sunday morning services held in the bush lasted for five hours and even then the people were reluctant to go home. On this particular morning I witnessed a rather amusing incident which again proves the earnestness of these dear people in their worship. We were squatting on mats on the ground under the shade of four large trees, our company numbering over one hundred. During the worship I noticed that something was causing amusement amongst the children and youngest members, so, following the direction of their gaze, I saw a big man directly under one of the trees whose hair seemed to have turned red overnight. On closer investigation I discovered that his hair was covered with red ants, which were apparently enjoying the flavour of his hair oil. Despite the fact that the ants were actually down to his forehead and ears, he had his eyes closed, singing and rejoicing in the Lord, quite unaware of the presence of his uninvited guests."

James's real ministry has always been waiting on God. In some ways, as leader, his position was a lonely one and this drove him to pray even more. As the Church grew, the Ghanaians would love him and serve him and be his friend, but they would never confront or challenge him. He chose to listen to God and was big enough to obey, even when it seemed to go against his best interests. If this had not been the case, the story of the Church might have been very different.

1 Adam McKeown, quoted in *History of the Church of Pentecost (West Africa)* (Church of Pentecost: Accra, 1987), p 15.

One day in 1942, James, on his way home from a trek, stopped at Cape Coast. A voice said to him, "You're finished in Winneba". He arrived home and he was just telling Sophia that he thought they would soon be moving when there was a great noise and the end wall of their house fell down! It was just after the rains and the increased war-time lorry traffic had loosened the mud outside their house, undermining the foundations. With this as confirmation, James and Phia duly set off for Cape Coast and another chapter.

# Chapter 5
# A woman among women

It is said that behind every great man is a woman, and James was the first to acknowledge that he could never have accomplished all he did without his wife.

It was Sophia who persuaded her husband to go to Africa in the first place and, once she arrived, she had a definite role of her own to play. She began by teaching the women housework and sewing, but by 1939 she was writing, "At Winneba, our last station, I found the women were not so interested in needlework, but were more anxious for the spiritual work; and when they heard of all the blessings, they were the more anxious for the baptism of the Holy Ghost and the blessings which would follow. They had no time for needlework, but for prayer (and indeed, oftentimes, they made me feel ashamed.) One woman storekeeper prayed from nine to twelve in the morning and from three to five in the afternoon, waiting for the baptism, and when it happened 'It poured out upon her.' A very high privilege and a great honour has been bestowed on us to minister to these dear women (though they are ignorant and not at all nice as we see them in heathen worship) but when we see them saved and filled with the Holy Ghost, they are very beautiful to us, and beautiful to God. We love them and our work. Praise His precious Name!"[1]

James would often leave his wife alone while he went off on trek and lamented, "I think I was a better missionary than I was a husband, but Sophia was not as happy about travelling and mixing with people as I was." Sophia found it harder to

1 "Nuggets from the Gold Coast," an address given by Sophia at the August 1939 convention of the Apostolic Church and recorded in *Riches of Grace* for that year.

make friends than James. It must have been lonely and frightening for her to be abandoned for weeks at a time in the early days, but she did not complain and she was always supportive of her husband. This was her top priority. Sophia believed in James. There were times when he may not have been as confident as he appeared, but she would encourage him when he was discouraged and had a very quiet influence on him all the time. She served James so he could spend time seeking God, as well as releasing him to evangelise and care for the ever-growing Church.

James was a tall, broad, powerful figure of a man. Sophia looked tiny and frail beside him, but how poised and elegant she was! This woman had lived in the tropics for years and yet she would not have looked out of place on the pages of a Paris magazine – only because she was an outstanding needlewoman. She could even do tailoring and make hats. Her face was attractive – her kind, gentle smile drew everyone to love her. James said that he only knew her to quarrel with anyone once in her life and that was under great provocation.

The Africans loved Sophia partly because she identified with them. She used local foodstuffs, such as cassava and *nkontomire,*[2] which most foreigners at the time would never have dreamt of cooking. Unusually, Africans felt free to pop in and out of the McKeowns' house, consuming tea and cake. Sophia's gift for hospitality extended to the little details – there would always be talc and hand-cream for visitors to use.

English missionaries were intrigued by the way Africans greeted the McKeowns. James was 'Papa' and Sophia was 'Mama'. Though they had no physical children of their own, thousands of Africans loved and respected the McKeowns as much as they did their own parents. Both the McKeowns had numerous children named after them. In Africa names are

2 African spinach-like vegetable

long and important – for example, one Ghanaian rejoices in the name of Miss Sophia McKeown Araba Poloa Paintsil – all because her parents wanted their daughter to grow up to be like Sophia.

Sophia might have seemed frail, but she took on a work-load which amazed even the hard-working African women. James said she was the cleanest girl in the countryside and did all her own housework, washing and ironing, allowing her house-girl, Gladys, to do only the sweeping. The only criticism voiced of her was that she was a little house-proud.

James sometimes took Sophia on trek if he felt the conditions would not be too rough, but was a little wary, because he knew that when they stayed with someone, she would lift the pillows and look under the bed. She might well have been excused. In a country where legs of food-cupboards are stood in little pots of kerosine to discourage ants, where cockroaches and weevils live quite happily in refrigerators, where snakes slip into houses, and where the lady drinking from the communion cup before you may have TB or worse – who would not be fastidious? Sophia showed she was prepared to lay down her life by staying there at all. A woman who prided herself on being neat and clean chose to live in a climate where Westerners regularly endure skin rashes of all types – from prickly heat on. Perhaps James was over-protective of her. Sophia's attitude, even on trek was that God knew Pastor James had a wife at his call, so God would take care of them wherever they went. She was prepared to overcome her natural fastidiousness and the Ghanaians appreciated this.

On trek, the McKeowns would find a village and sit under a shade tree. There they would sing and James would begin to preach, but apart from some curious children giggling behind the bushes, no-one listened. Then, one time, Sophia had an idea. As they sang, 'Oh, God is good', she jumped up and began to dance. The people had never seen a white woman dancing before and soon the whole village had turned out to watch the strange phenomenon. They stayed on to hear the Gospel and believed. James asked, with a twinkle in his eye, "Would she have learned *that* at Bible school!"

Later, as a typical Church meeting got under way, Sophia's role was not limited to ministering to women. First she had a message in tongues which James interpreted. Then she prayed, and what a prayer! It was not long but somehow everyone knew that she had touched God. During the lengthy worship James himself stayed on the platform, almost as if he were the still centre of the meeting. Sophia, neat and precise, headed the line of sisters as they moved out in dance – one white woman from an Irish Presbyterian background leading hundreds of swaying African ladies!

James might preach for over an hour, then some of the Africans would say, "Give your wife a turn". Usually he beckoned Sophia to stand up and she began speaking in a clear voice. Her words were simple, direct and practical as she urged the people to live the holy life to which God had called them. A woman preacher was so unusual that missionaries often asked James about it. He said that he had always encouraged his wife to preach. At open air meetings, crowds would be drawn just because a white woman was speaking.

When he was first in Africa, James found that he could not trust men with money. Women seemed more honest and James resorted to having two women watch each collection bowl, to see people did not take out more than they put in. James said that according to the teaching of the Apostolic Church back home, he should have been looking for men to work with, but they did not seem to be forthcoming at this stage. It was women who came and were baptised in the Holy Spirit; women who gave money and committed their time and women who prayed. "I don't know what the women in St Paul's day were doing wrong," said James, "But I retained my own mind and judgement. We did not let them run away with it, just gave them their place and the gifts of the Spirit were there and in use."

Women often found it easier to receive the Holy Spirit than did the men. One pastor laughed as he remembered, "Some of us were put through a lot of prayer and fasting... It took me about two years and women were falling to the left and right, filled with the Holy Ghost, speaking in tongues, and I opened my eyes and thought, 'Oh God, why?' "

In market places throughout the region, women were telling stories about what was happening, so even when James preached in a new place, people were curious to come and listen. Women were even opening assemblies at that time – Dunkwa on Offin, Kumasi, Sekondi, Takoradi – the women went to all the key places from Saltpond, 'taking the fire down' as they put it. If James had his way, most of the human credit for the foundation of the Church of Pentecost would go to women like Mrs Obo.

The place of women in African society is often a lowly one, but the Africans recognised that James was not a fool in his attitude to them. They said a chief whose wife was on his side could weather many storms, but if she was against him and trouble came, everyone else would leave as fast as rats from a sinking ship. Even Kwame Nkrumah, when he wanted support, did not bother much with the men, but enlisted women of the market to his cause. Just so, the women stood by James. "Was not the wisdom of God with me?" he asked.

It is hard for us today to realise how revolutionary was James' attitude to women in the Church. He was always in trouble, especially from the Apostolics, who gave women very little scope at all. When Herbert Cousen, the missionary chairman of the Apostolic Church, heard alarming reports and came out to the Gold Coast to see what was going on with the women, all he could say was, "Carry on, James, it works!" James stressed submission of wives to husbands and other important Scriptural principles, but refused to be pressurised by the extra rules other churches had laid down. Women were free to reach their full potential in Christ. Had they been stifled, would the Church ever have grown as it did?

It was right back in 1938 that the Women's Movement was started in Ghana. It echoed that of the UK Apostolic Church and James always considered it to be of great significance, a prime tool for evangelism and for teaching the new women converts how to live according to God's way. The Women's Movement, with its slogan, 'Holiness to the Lord', has grown to be a major wing of the Church. It has its own huge conventions as well as weekly meetings. Sophia was a great influence on the Movement. They said, "her axiom in life which she lived out to the full and inspired the women to live by was, 'Wives, submit to your husbands as to the Lord' (Eph 5 v22 NIV). This is still being sounded in towns and villages throughout Ghana and husbands are being won for Christ as the result of transformation in the lives of their wives, and homes have become a living testimony to the power of the Gospel. Our mother lived out Scriptures as well as taught them. We women could happily follow Mama as she followed Christ."[3]

Sophia was never the Movement's leader and the Africans appreciated the fact that she did not seek to dominate, but rather encouraged them to assume responsibility. Nevertheless, she did all she could to help. She wrote pamphlets and syllabuses, many of which are in use to this day. Sophia knew her Bible and often spoke from it about marriage, about how to live free from sin and other very practical matters. Sophia collected about her the more educated women such as Mrs Obo and Mrs Adams, and such was her influence that even some of her house-girls went on to become pastor's wives.

3 Women's Movement tribute in Sophia's memorial service pamphlet. (Quote slightly changed for clarity.)

Sophia died six years before James, in 1983. Her affect on the Church may be gauged by this piece written in 1987 by a young deaconess. Part of it, translated, said, "There were times when, because of our salvation, you kept vigil, fasted and prayed in support of the work your husband was doing. You were white, but for our sakes, you became black. You ate food you had never tasted at home. You made long journeys, went through thick bushes and forests, climbed and descended hills, crossed dangerous rivers, both day and night, following your lord (James McKeown) in search of us who were lost and you brought us to Christ. There was no trace of racial discrimination in you. Sophia, you merit the accolade, 'Virtuous Wife'.[4] The present day leaders of the Church of Pentecost acknowledge that both James and Sophia laid a foundation of truth in them, saying, "We are leaders because we were led and teachers because we were taught."

4 Sister Angelina Fraikue, "The Virtuous Wife", *Pentecost Fire* issue 84 (1987): p 16.

# Chapter 6
# Roots in Africa, Worship and Giving

Cape Coast was once the capital of the Gold Coast and is still an important place, especially for education, but at the time James moved there, the Apostolics met in a corrugated-iron shed in the worst area of town. James had virtually no money and knew that finding living accommodation in Cape Coast would not be easy. He also knew God had told him to move there, and in that sense felt the problem was God's responsibility. At last a Methodist lady said she had a spare room, but not many days after the McKeowns moved in, she came banging at the door. "Your room is where the ancestor spirits stay," she informed James. "I am afraid they are troubled by your praying – you will have to go!"

A friend knew of somewhere else which might be suitable but the man who owned it did not like missionaries. Undaunted, the penniless James told the owner his Father was a millionaire. The man was so impressed he let James have the top floor of Aboom House at a very reasonable rent. It had two apartments, which left plenty of room to house other Apostolic missionaries who came to join the McKeowns later. So God, the 'millionaire', had provided.

Meanwhile, an Italian builder had taken over the Methodist lady's room and, because it was war time, hoarded petrol there. A few days after the McKeowns moved out the whole building went up in flames and that was the last anyone heard of the ancestor spirits!

In Cape Coast, as in Winneba, James made a base from which he went on treks into the bush. Facing criticism for this policy from missionary headquarters in Bradford, he replied, "What use is a head without a body?" These treks were an adventure story in their own right. James's only transport was an old pedal bike. "You should have seen him pushing it with the chain broken!" chuckled one Ghanaian. He would normally travel longer distances by 'mammy lorry', the erratic local equivalent of a bus service. A whole day might be spent by the roadside, hoping for a lift on one of these ramshackle vehicles, which was bulging already with husky African women and all their market goods. Squashed on wooden benches with humidity high, temperatures exceeding one hundred degrees in the shade and red dust covering everything, it was not the most comfortable form of travel.

James must have been relieved when, after the war, he took delivery of his own transport – a pick-up truck! He had never driven anything other than a tram before and had only one day to practise manoeuvring before his driving test. The examiner pronounced, "I could fail you, McKeown, you did not keep near enough in to the side!" James explained he had been used to driving trams in Glasgow and the official smiled. "I'm from Kelvinside," he said, "you've passed!"

Transport or no, away from the roads, James had to walk. Other missions worked near the coast, or the main highways, but James would tramp five, six, even ten days into the snake-infested bush with Pastor Anaman. The fact that James was one of the few people willing to do this explains why his Church now has so many assemblies. People living in remote areas had never heard the Gospel before – they had probably never seen a white man either. Conditions were decidedly rough but James did not mind where he went. He often used government rest-houses, but even here he had to provide his own bedding, food and cooking utensils. One night he might lodge in a large house with nice, respectable Presbyterians: the next alongside all the creepy crawlies in a mud hut. Wild beasts howled outside, but James was never afraid. Pastor Safo, the Ghanaian who succeeded as chairman of the Church, was amazed, "James travelled constantly and if you saw the places where he slept ... I do not think I could sleep in such places!" These things just did not seem important to James – he said he would do anything to get on with the work.

The strength James had developed working on the farm during his youth stood him in good stead now. He was rarely tired and reckoned he could outlast two African pastors. Not even the heat bothered him. In this steamy part of the world, where people sweat just sitting in the shade, several baths a day are the norm. Sometimes this meant James joined the village men for a swim in the river, much to their surprise and delight. If a bucket were available, he would take a 'shower' by hanging it from a tree, soaping himself all over and using the water for a final rinse. Africans who had never seen a white man before were curious and James had to get used to women peeping through the palm branches!

Expeditions involved danger. Early on, James and a team of workers were nearly drowned in the Bonsa river. Once, in a drought, James was forced to rely on raw guinea-fowl eggs for moisture – and this was the first time he had tasted eggs since one turned his stomach at the age of eleven. Another time his face was stung by a swarm of bees. He carried on, despite the swelling and blisters, saying better to risk his life for the African than to stay at home where there wasn't much work to do.

James had always been one to grin at danger. Even as a boy he loved the sort of wind that brought roofing slates and chimneys crashing down. One day in 1939, James was walking through Winneba when he heard a strange rumbling noise. He wondered why everybody was running and shouting until he realised that this was an earthquake – and a big one. Returning to his house, James lay on his bed, watching cracks appear in the walls as they shook. Phia was terrified but James reasoned, "It's not every day you get the chance to enjoy an earthquake!"

During the 1939-45 war, James and Sophia were

effectively marooned in the Gold Coast. Whereas other missions sent supplies to their people, no parcels arrived for the Apostolics. They tried boiling corn, but after two or three hours, it was as hard as ever. No-one had told them it must first be pounded and the husk removed. Today, missionaries in Ghana would keep everything – even flour and cornflakes – away from insects in the deep freeze, but the McKeowns did not even have a refrigerator. Unlike other missionaries they had no car and only a rented house, but this did not bother them. In the end their comparative poverty was to prove more of an advantage than otherwise – the Africans could relate to people who had needs and found a dignity in giving. By contrast it was said of some American missionaries, "They don't write letters, they sign cheques." On occasions James stayed with these men and they could not understand why eggs, chickens, and fruit were constantly arriving at the door for James. "The Africans never give us anything," they complained, as they watched James struggle off to the next village, clutching armfuls of yams, six pound pineapples and a couple of live chickens.

James asked some of his African friends, real men of God and leaders in the Church, why they treated him differently from other white people. They explained, "We used to feel shy and afraid even sitting near a white man. We felt in our minds they were so superior to us that even when we got near them we felt timid, but you, Pastor, from the beginning you got yourself very low. We see how you like children and embrace them; you are easily accessible and do not place yourself high up in the air. You are so simple to all of us and anybody can go to you. We have always been in and out of your house and you sit down with us and eat and share. By these things you win the heart of the people!" "Yes," remembered James, "We had some happy times together."

"And then," went on the Africans, "you travelled together with us in the bush – the bush is not like Accra. See – there you and the wife are eating cassava – our lowest form of food.

You white men were our colonial masters, and we thought of you as very high – if you would eat our food, if you could come down to the level of a servant, then we know it means something to you." One of the men laughed, "You did not want to hurt the people you stayed with – you would eat any food that was brought before you, because you said these things are from people's hearts and we should not be ignoring them. And because you and your wife humbled yourselves to our level, this brought people in." "When we saw that you wanted to be with us and not with other missionaries," added another, "we came to trust you with everything."

Later, whenever the McKeowns returned from furlough, the quayside was jammed with excited crowds. The people on the boat had never seen a reception like this laid on for anyone and wondered who was the VIP attracting all this attention? They had their cameras at the ready and could not understand why all the fuss was centred on a quiet, unobtrusive couple called McKeown. Though James could laugh at such things, he never liked being fêted. Later, he used to say, "Don't tell them I'm arriving at the airport!" So many queued to welcome him, they caused a traffic jam right through Accra.

James never understood how some missionaries could talk behind the African's backs one day and preach to them the next. James felt even listening to such talk would spoil his mind and because he chose to associate almost exclusively with Africans, they trusted him. Both James and Sophia often wore the local dress and really came to be regarded as Africans who happened to have white skin. Yet in the beginning there was a sense in which James felt he could not get near them and throughout the early period, the one thing he longed for more than anything else was true fellowship.

James began to fast and pray – specifically that he might feel a closeness in spirit with at least one African. One night, before a meeting, God gave him nothing to preach on except the word 'prayer'. As he announced it would be a prayer meeting that night, James hoped the people would really pray, not just talk. As James prayed out loud, he felt that in some way his spirit entered into a young man called J. Cofie Quaye, with whom he had stayed when visiting Winneba. Quaye then prophesied in a remarkable way. He went on to enter the ministry in 1943, when he was 28 years old, remaining in it 41 years; he pioneered the preaching of the Gospel in many areas of the Gold Coast, became the Church's first prophet and later an apostle. James could never have accomplished all he did alone, but once he realised the Spirit of God could overcome all the cultural differences and make him truly one with the Africans, he began to find men into whom he could put something of his own spirit and burden. Church growth followed.

Europeans thought him mad to trust Africans with people and with money, but his real expectation that God would work in the true converts bore fruit. He wrote, "This has been our aim in allowing the work in Africa to retain its native characteristics and it has resulted in producing some of the finest Christians I have yet met. Let there be no mistaking the high standard of both the work and the members, for despite the absence of legalism and the background of heathenism, there are emerging many who are attracted to the Spirit of Jesus, men and women of like heart and character."[1]

Perhaps the keynote was respect. James respected the local culture, except where it went against the Word of God. He was never interested in promoting himself or his own culture, only Jesus. Recently, a lady meeting James for the first time could tell by his accent that he came from Coatbridge in Scotland. James explained, "Despite all my

1 James McKeown quoted in *History of the Church of Pentecost (West Africa)* (Church of Pentecost: Accra, 1987), p11.

years in West Africa and Northern Ireland, I have kept my Scottish speech and ways, as is the right of every man. I am James and I never go to imitate anybody. I did not come to change the Africans from being African: I told them they should be proud of being African. Jesus changes people's character, not their nationality. I taught them the Bible, got them to know Jesus and told them if God is giving children, He hasn't to send to England for a nose to put on an African!"

James loved the colourful clothes which Ghanaian women wear. Typically, they comprise a three-piece garment, with each piece made from the same vivid cotton print. The first part is a frilly top, then, over a long skirt, the women drape a rectangular cloth – which can be taken off and used for carrying babies, or shopping! James watched as women danced out in a meeting, unwound their rectangular cloths and swirled them in the dust. One of the men explained that the women swept the ground before their chief in this way, as he passed in procession, seated on his palanquin. Now they were doing the same in honour of Jesus.

James began to think about worship. When he was speaking in the UK, he observed that people found worship difficult and strange in comparison to these Africans. Was it because they no longer had a model for it in their everyday lives? Who, apart from God, did they revere? James could see that these Africans lived more as people did in biblical times. They were not isolated in their homes: they made their own entertainment outdoors, naturally involving the whole community. Festivals, weddings, funerals, or just something to do in the evening – there were so many occasions for drumming and dancing. James frowned. He knew this was not always good – it could lead to immorality. But what about the ceremonies to honour the Chiefs? James began to see how certain words, dances and gestures which had evolved for this purpose could be directed towards the worship of God.

A few years later Afua Kuma stood in a convention and spoke for twenty minutes without a break. James's translator struggled – her words did not readily convert to English. They were part of a specialised vocabulary normally used in praise of the chief, whereby his 'names were named', for example, 'Lord of a thousand villages,' 'Mighty in battle' and so on.

Afua was reciting one of her praise poems about the names of God. The mother in law of one of the Church of Pentecost's apostles, she farmed in the forests of the Kwahu plateau and she could not read or write. Yet her words reminded James of the Psalms – the imagery she used to describe God was drawn from everyday things.

*"Damfo-Adu:"* she said, "Great Clever One,
We rely on you as the tongue relies on the mouth.
The great Rock we hide behind:
the great forest canopy that gives cool shade,
the Big Tree which lifts its vines
to peep at the heavens,
the magnificent Tree whose dripping leaves
encourage the luxuriant growth below."[2]

My enemies say they will kill me
but Jesus is the Chief of Police,
and my enemies have fled,
leaving me in peace."[3]

James listened as the drummers began. Music and rhythm seemed natural to Africans – some of the best drummers were young boys. He looked around at the children. A few

2 Her words were later taped, then translated from the Twi language into a booklet. Afua Kuma, *Jesus of the Deep Forest,* translated by Fr John Kirby, SVD (Asempa: Accra, 1981), p 5.
3 Ibid. p 18.

little ones were curled up on the benches, fast asleep, but for most, the worship was too exciting. Song leaders perspired as they led the worship and groups of women played tambourines, dancing at the same time. Others had calabashes – instruments from the north of the country – hollow hemispheres made from gourds, with cowrie shells strung round the outside. They threw and caught and twirled these in time with the tambourines.

There was a change of pace as singing groups from three different assemblies came up on the platform to sing in a variety of styles. Soon thousands of white hankies were being waved in the air as the people praised God with total abandon. James smiled – it was quite a sight! The meeting changed gear again as a pastor read a few words of Scripture and called them to worship. Everyone closed their eyes and either sang or spoke in tongues. It did not last very long but, thought James, such times always seemed to bring the presence of God particularly near. James was pleased. Despite all the vibrant life in these meetings he never felt uncomfortable or that things were getting out of hand, and there were times when it was as though the Spirit of God came down and His glory filled the place.

Next it was James's turn to preach. He found his sermons were interrupted occasionally by some African who stood up to sing a song which took up some point from his preaching. Then, as one or two dived for pencil and paper to write the new song down, the rest would join in, harmonising as only Africans can. This was how many of the songs they sing regularly began.

After James spoke, a five year old Ewe (pronounced 'evveh') boy stood on a chair in front of thousands and sang a song into the microphone. One of the pastors on the platform behind could contain himself no longer. Grinning with delight, he started to dance, then all the Ewes surged forward, with comical backwards-elbow movements. Still balanced on his chair, the boy could not move his feet. As if to compensate, he almost dislocated his shoulders as he moved his arms in time to the music, for all the world like an enthusiastic chick leading a crowd of plump mother hens.

What will the worship in heaven be like, James wondered, when every tribe and nation brings their own expression of praise to Jesus? "I thought I was going out to teach," he thought, "but I've been taught. Phia and I started singing and clapping hands but we did not have to teach the Africans to dance."

Then the people began to sing in the language of a different tribe, and all that tribe came out for their special dance. Children joined in, dancing, clapping and singing. James thought about the way outsiders reacted when they saw the Church worshipping like this. "They are always taken aback at the way the Africans really enter into worship," he reflected. "We have such a lot to learn back in the UK!"

Most outsiders who have visited the Church of Pentecost have found the exuberant praise such a joy they hardly notice the hard wooden benches, even through a five hour Communion service. For long-stay Westerners, it might not be so easy to sit through the frequent meetings – simply because they are tuned to the African rather than the European and everything seems to take three times as long as it does in the West. James, though, could sit for hours. "I would wait on the Lord in my own way, and never found it a burden," he said.

Altogether, the Church has made quite a contribution to preserving Ghana's cultural heritage – their creative music is often played on the country's radio. While many churches in Ghana now imitate the worship of the Church of Pentecost, it was not so in the early days, when it was fashionable to appear European. It was thought that James's Church – which not only allowed clapping, drumming, dancing and speaking in tongues, but also met in old sheds – was obviously for simple village people who knew no better. In the Gold Coast of the 1940's most churches banned hand clapping (never mind drumming and dancing.) Such things were considered crude and uncivilised. Instead, robed choirs sang nineteenth century English hymns to organ accompaniment, "But there was no grace in it," commented James. Any educated African who became involved in James's Church had to face strong disapproval from his or her family. It meant great financial sacrifice and loss of reputation. Paradoxically, it was not easy for this new African Church to take root in its own soil, in a time when it was so obviously different from any other church.

From the beginning, James wanted the Church in Ghana to be indigenous, with African culture, ministry and finance. He saw that it would be difficult to grow an English oak in Ghana. Unless you created a special environment, the tree would be unlikely to survive. He concluded the same was true of the church. A local 'species', at home in its culture, should grow, reproduce and spread: a church with foreign cultural roots was more likely to struggle. Strangely enough, it was James' lack of money which worked in several ways to help achieve his aim.

If the Church's policy of keeping to the local culture was later vindicated – how did their poverty lead to a financially self-sufficient Church? More than that – if James started with £10 in his pocket, how did he ever build a Church at all?

James did not waste any time worrying about material possessions, or even where the next meal was coming from. He knew God who had called him – He would provide. As for the Africans, James considered it was his part to help them to know God – then God would look after them. When James preached, people were described as not just being converted, but as "being set on fire for Jesus." He told them, "This fire will mean sacrifice, it will burn right into your pockets and money will be coming out." At the beginning, no one in the Church was used to giving. Even those at Akroso, who were behind James in most ways, balked at the Apostolic teaching on tithing. As people became full of vision though, they began to follow James's example of sacrificial giving and trust in God. One of his favourite sayings was, "You don't need to teach Jacob to tithe." James was referring to the passage in Genesis 28 where Jacob dreamt about angels on the ladder to heaven. Afterwards, Jacob burst out, "And of all that you give me I will give you a tenth." (Genesis 28:22 NIV) James concluded from this that if someone is spiritual, he will do as God wants, but if he has not been touched by God, no amount of teaching will change his attitudes and behaviour.

The early pastors had little financial support. James said they should follow Jesus's teaching and accept whatever food was offered to them as they preached the Gospel on the road. Becoming a pastor meant giving up everything for a very hard life and many who were called took several years before they were prepared to make those sacrifices. Some gave up good jobs in gold or diamond mines. Even today, pastors' salaries are small and their lives hard. The supreme test, though, came in the 1950s. The Church was involved in litigation which went against them and James asked his pastors to forgo their salaries until the debt was paid. This they did for a whole year saying, "It doesn't worry us, we're happy. Better to have McKeown leading us than physical advantages with no salvation in it. He's making us be firm and prove God is true."

James built a 'Do It Yourself Church' – one which could feed itself both with ministry and with finance. Some other missions had large sums coming from home base – James even found one congregation bribed to attend with tins of sardines! The pressure to accept outside help was always there. Another Apostolic missionary, who joined James during the time he was at Cape Coast, caused trouble by promising funds from the UK. James countered, "Shame on you Africans! One of these days you will be shouting for self-government, why not take it now? If you accept money from the white man you will always be tied to his apron strings. I have not come to Africa to create beggars but sons of God. So put it to the test. If God is responsible for what has happened then He will provide, if James McKeown, then he will be responsible. Take your self-government now from God!"

It is not riches that make a church. When Cecil Cousen and his wife Jean visited James's Church for a week in 1947, Jean wrote in her diary, "This evening we attended the meeting in Tafo where we have a good assembly. The meeting was held outside with all the congregation sitting on benches. We sat facing them with a table in front of us, and a large kerosene lamp as a means of lighting. We had the usual battery of insects in attendance!! After the meeting most of the congregation walked home with us in the dark, one or two carrying tilley lamps to light us on our way, and all singing their lovely haunting native choruses. It was one of the most delightful experiences I have had in West Africa and one I shall always remember."

By insisting the Church was self-supporting right from the beginning, James showed his trust not only in God but also in the Africans. He made them stand on their own feet. During my visit to Ghana in 1987 they explained, "James caused us to know that the God who called us would give us means. Today we see all the buildings, all the money that is flowing through the Church and it makes our hearts glad – even some rich men see it and believe God is true." But where did all this money came from in a poor country like Ghana? The chairman of the Church of Pentecost smiled when faced with this question, "Of a truth, it is beyond our understanding where the money comes from." The answer has to be that God provides. He loves a cheerful giver and honours the people's attitudes. For example, one young pastor is always giving away his goats. Strangely, when his goats breed, instead of normal single births, they have twins or triplets.

At one time, the Church was criticized, because, unlike other denominations, it made no contribution to education or social welfare. James's priority was always evangelism and social benefits accrued where people's lives changed. For example, criminals and drunkards became model citizens. Right back in 1945, James explained his vision. "Our policy for the future is to put the claims of Jesus Christ first, on this ground: establish churches and as the church is able to bear the burden without endangering her health as a spiritual power, we will open schools for the education of the youth." This has in fact happened. In 1954, salaries accounted for 95% of the Church's expenditure, but by 1982, salaries made up less than 14%. A large proportion of the Church's income is now spent on schools, agricultural and social projects to help the nation.

The Church's recent balance sheets are amazing. Targets for giving are, more often than not, exceeded. During an Easter convention, perhaps sixteen offerings are taken up and the people give with as much enthusiasm at the end as they did at the beginning. All this in a situation where an average day's wage buys one pineapple and a man would have to work a week to earn enough for a chicken. If we in the West were generous on this scale, what could we not see done for the Kingdom?

In 1982, the Church's financial target of eight million cedis was exceeded by 50% and that of the missionary offerings by 41% – a remarkable achievement when conditions in the country were taken into account. These were the dark days before the economic crisis and near-famine of 1983. Norman Barnes found many of his friends at that time just half their normal weight. No-one was eating more than once every other day, yet he never heard a word of complaint. They came to meetings full of smiles and one Sunday, cheerfully gave to four different offerings, one of which was for the poor and needy! Norman felt that the attitude of these people, together with their prayer, might well have so touched the heart of God that he intervened to change the gloomy outlook of the country. (Ghana went from famine to bumper harvests in just one year.)

I had never visited a Third World country before I went to Ghana and worried about my reactions on being brought face to face with real poverty for the first time. I found that poverty is not pleasant, but it need not rob people of everything as materialism does. It was not in Ghana that I felt physically sick and disgusted, but afterwards, in a shopping mall in England. In Ghana, I cried often, not because of people's poverty, but because of the extraordinary generosity they showed, wherever we went. When as a group, we were provided with bottles of Coke which cost the pastor two days wages, it was not easy to drink. When the back of our van was filled with fruit, vegetables and eggs, when we were put up in a rest-house at their expense, fed, given money and various souvenirs as well, when we saw the conditions they lived in and the sacrifice they had made – it was difficult to keep smiling, look pleased and say thank you. This, according to their culture, is what you must do to make them happy.

James, like us, found it easier to give than to receive. "One thing I've had to learn," he said, "is when I'm given something not to say, 'Oh, you shouldn't do that!' but to beam my thank-yous. There is nothing mean about the Church of Pentecost. They gave Sophia £2,300 when she returned to Ireland in 1974, which paid for half our retirement bungalow. When I objected, they told me, 'It's not for you, it's for your wife.'" James looked around his home in wonder, "There can't be many white people who can say Africans gave them all this."

"All this" is how God has rewarded and honoured everything that happened in Ghana, but it was James' poverty, his willingness to live as they lived, which helped him be accepted, not as the big white chief, but as a servant-leader who bestowed dignity on his people. As they have learnt to rely on God's provision, this Church's roots have been forced deep into God's love. They avoided the easy option of becoming a parasite on another tree, which is one reason they have stood firm and are in a healthy state today. The Church of Pentecost might be described as a tree whose leaves and shoots and roots are African – everything, from their worship to their administration, looks and feels Ghanaian. They are justly proud of being beholden only to God.

# Chapter 7
# Born to Reproduce – The Evangelists

3,000 local churches from nothing in fifty years. The Church of Pentecost snowballed because spreading the Gospel was its top priority, but on the boat when he was going to Africa for the first time, James was shocked when he heard other missionaries say, "Don't tell people you preach." Had evangelism become socially unacceptable, he wondered?

James learnt that missionaries had arrived in the Gold Coast up to a hundred years before. They made many converts, but then became involved in educational, administrative and medical projects, all of which required money. In order to raise it they engaged in trade. Most of their resources were directed away from the purpose for which they had come – evangelism.[1] James realised that some of his own later success came because he was building on the good work of the first missionaries, but that they had now left a gap which he was filling. He told Debrunner, "Your other missionaries and your African pastors and collaborators labour and sweat with the school – and then you leave the people on their own, neglecting evangelism – and thus we can harvest where you have sown."[2]

1 Hans W Debrunner wrote in his standard *History of Christianity in Ghana* (Waterville Publishing House: Accra, 1967) p 325, "Many missionaries of the established Churches felt indeed that the overburdening of the missionaries with educational and administrative work between 1920 and 1950 was a very mixed blessing... One of them said that this was what he had always wanted to do in Ghana and what the missionaries had done there before the First World War: 'Just to evangelize'."
2 *Ibid.*

At the beginning, one District Commissioner, surprised a missionary was setting up neither clinics nor schools, asked James what he was doing in the country. James knew he had come to preach the Gospel to the Gold Coast and beyond, but even so, the question set him thinking. "I am digging wells," he said. "Abraham was not content with surface water, which can be polluted. He sunk wells until he struck the rock – and the rock is Jesus. The Philistines filled in the wells, but Isaac dug them again, as you can read in Genesis 21:25 and 26:15-22. I do not want to make people decide to become Christians in their minds, because then any change in them will be on the surface. I will not be content until these people see the Cross and are broken there, until they fall in love with Jesus."

"Surely they have other needs?" asked the District Commissioner. "That may be," replied James, "But I have nothing of myself to give them. What the Africans need is not education: they need rivers of living water flowing out of their hearts and lives. Once we have a strong Church of people who really know Jesus and the Holy Spirit, then everything else will follow."

A God-given opportunity to reach a new group of people with the Gospel came six months after James went to live in Winneba. He was preaching in Akroso marketplace when some men came up to him and said, "We are a church 3,000 strong and a prophet said that a white man would come and teach us the good way." They explained that their leader, John Nackabah, had seen a vision of a tall Englishman coming along to teach them. Noticing James, Nackabah pointed straight to him, "This is the man I saw in my dream." On the strength of this, his church asked James to come and help them, promising to pay his fare and all expenses.

James took as interpreter a young man from Akroso called S. R. Asomaning, who afterwards became his first African pastor. Together they travelled by mammy lorry and train as far as Prestea in the Western Region. As the train pulled away, James wondered why there was so much singing, shouting and dancing. "These are the band come to meet and greet you," he was told. James felt bemused and not a little shy. They took him right off into the bush to a little mining village and James was very glad when he arrived at the home where he was to lodge, for a welcome bath and cup of tea!

After this, he was taken to a large mud building. 3,000 people overflowed its doors and hung out of its windows. Most were all shouting and dancing. James had never before spoken to such a large crowd away from home and again felt very shy, especially as they seemed to regard him as a kind of battery sent fully charged from heaven! As soon as they touched him they appeared to be charged with power and started jumping about. They barked like dogs and croaked like frogs. "What is this?" James asked, but was told "Don't say anything!"

James explained all he learnt about the background of Nackabah's group in an article he wrote at the time. "This Church was the fruit of the ministry of a man named Prophet Wade Harris, a native of Liberia who, during the years of the Great War, obeyed the voice of God and went throughout the Ivory Coast and part of the Gold Coast, calling upon the people to forsake their idols and turn to God. In some cases, his influence was greater than that of the world's famous evangelists. He told them to build churches and buy Bibles. 'A white man will come and teach you' was his final word to the people."[3] That was in 1914.

After the war ended, they were still left alone, despite asking for missionaries. By the time James reached them in 1938 all sorts of confusion had set in, because although the people had some experience of God and had burnt their fetishes, they had heard the Gospel only in part. Calling themselves 'The Church of the Twelve Apostles', this group

3 Pastor J McKeown, "Gathering Gold in the Gold Coast", *Herald of Grace* (1939): p 41.

claimed to hold the same beliefs as the Methodists. The Bible was used – but not for reading – it was waved at people who wanted to be baptised or healed!

In Ghana today, there are hundreds of churches or cults like this which mix elements of Christianity with traditional religions. They are often independent African groups, with a heavy emphasis on healing, prophecy and the supernatural and like to be known as 'Spiritual' churches.

On his second night in the remote village, James could not preach because the women were shouting. Again James asked "What is this?" and was told it was the power of the Holy Spirit. "Not the Holy Spirit I know," replied James, "He doesn't bark like a dog and croak like a frog!" James felt they were educationally further back than others he had worked with. The dog and frog noises were a shock, but his African companions urged him not to interrupt, saying, "Pastor, softly, softly catch the monkey!"

After a day or two they quietened down a little and James was able to preach. They responded so well he baptised 200 by immersion. He was told that Friday was their special day. He should come to their meeting and take note of what he felt about it, but not interfere. In the early morning sunshine, a great row of people stretched out to his right, all dressed up for the occasion, wearing white hats and playing instruments. "These be prophets," he was told, "as they sing and play, the power of God will come down." To James's left was a similar long row, this time with large enamel basins of water on their heads. As these people danced they were drenched with water, which others replenished from the river by the bucketful. James was puzzled. "Don't you know the Scripture?" he was asked, "I will pour water upon him that is thirsty, and floods upon the dry ground?"[4] They thought that the Spirit came down into the water and, as it shook all over the people, they would be healed and demons would leave.

4 Isaiah 44:3 AV

After hours of frenzied drumming and dancing, many of the people seeking healing were in a trance-like state.

Then, a good looking, nicely dressed girl started a big dance, threw her basin down, had a jumping fit, took off nearly all her clothes and lay on the ground. James thought, "Whatever am I doing here looking at this!" He had promised not to interfere and so had to observe as a 'prophet' commanded ten spirits to come out of her. It was not a pleasant experience! Later he found that the issue was really about which man the girl should marry. This was the sort of thing he was up against, and he concluded there was extensive fornication among the so-called prophets and no evidence of real Christianity.

James would not give up but stayed in the village right over Christmas 1938, preaching at all times of the day and far into the night. God confirmed his words with miracles. At the end of six weeks, 1,288 souls accepted Jesus Christ as their personal Saviour and were baptised in water.

James then spent one week with Sophia before he went back to the village for another seven. "I appreciated my wife," he said, "Poor Phia! How would you like to be married to a man like that? But I did not want to bring her to these places, far in the bush."

Back in the village, James established companies of people willing to pioneer a work. However, problems began to arise. The local men worked in the diamond and gold mines and also grew rice. They often had several wives who helped on their farms. When James began to teach "One man, one wife," they asked if he would allow them just two. James replied, "The Bible does not say that, so please, if I endorse number two, who will endorse numbers three and four? The Scripture says no and it is no!" Many left but some elders from the Church of the Twelve Apostles stayed with them and a new assembly was started at a place called Wassa Simpa which continues to this day. However the rest of them could not or would not conform to God's standards of sexual behaviour.

Eunice Addison, one of James's earliest African converts, explained how it is only the grace of God which enlightens Ghana. "In a bush area, when a family goes to farm they will form a line, the father and mother leading with their head loads – they will follow paths already cut and not divert to the left or right. So their minds follow. In that area of Western Region very few had any education and their conscience told them things which might not necessarily be right. If they knew one thing, it was very hard for them to move on to another thing. They were very happy to hear the good news but – just as it was when Jesus preached about eating his flesh and drinking his blood after the feeding of the 5000, many went away – so it happened here, over the issues of polygamy and fornication."

At first, evangelism was slow – there were often two steps forward and one back. However, James found that villages right out in the bush had their own form of civilisation which could help spread the Gospel. Anyone arriving in a village was expected first to go to its chief, to state the purpose of his visit and enquire about the well-being of the community. James likened making friends with the chief to Matthew 12:24 AV, "Else how can one enter into a stong man's house, and spoil his goods, except he first bind the strong man?" A friendly chief would beat the gong-gong, summoning all of his subjects to hear what the evangelists had to say.

James wrote in 1941 about two visits to remote villages. "I had for company my interpreter and my cook. The first village we called at gave us a royal welcome and I was taken straight to the chief's house where I was to stay. I had to state my reason for coming to the village and my message. The chief, a fine looking man, could converse quite freely with me in English. While I was speaking to him I noticed charms and medicines for the protection of the village and its chief. Upon looking round this village, the failure of these charms and medicines to achieve their desired effect is painfully apparent, for there are many sick in the village walking round covered with sores and many lepers. The people here are slaves to fear. I set about declaring the glorious Gospel of freedom and they and their chief listened attentively and rejoiced at the message, but it is very hard for them to give up their superstitious beliefs and they wanted both the charms and the Gospel. There were also those who for years had been slaves to sinful pleasures and they found it very hard to cast these aside, but, in spite of all the difficulties in the way, 29 people in the village surrendered to the Saviour and were baptised in water, many having received the Baptism of the Holy Ghost."[5]

James stayed a few more days, before responding to calls for help from the church in another village. He set off by train and then managed to catch a lift on a lorry, but when it dropped him off in the late afternoon, he still had a six mile walk through the bush. There was nothing for it but to leave his luggage and race to reach his destination. Dusk falls quickly in the tropics. Long before there was any sign of the village, James could hardly see where he was going. As he stumbled over roots and boulders his thoughts turned to other things which might lurk unseen – poisonous snakes, for example. Then, flickering ahead of him, he saw tiny lights. Some villagers were coming out to greet him, and never had a welcome seemed more sweet!

Next day, James had a problem. He was due to speak to a Church meeting, but the only clothes he had were in a terrible state after his journey. The village men brought him a long piece of colourful cloth such as they themselves wore, draped around them, and so it was that James preached for the first time in African dress. In his article to the Apostolic Church back home James wrote, "One of the things I love about these bush towns is the freedom from many of the formalities which bind one in the more enlightened towns."

5 Pastor J McKeown, "Reports from the Gold Coast", *Herald of Grace* (Jan 1941): p5.

He continued, "After a few days, I found that, although forty of the people wanted to be baptised, they knew nothing of the grace of God. The idea prevails in them that they will undergo some change in baptism, as though there were some virtue in the water to change them. Many will give themselves for baptism and after go back to a life of sin. We have to make it very clear to them that no outward form of baptism will bring the spirit of God to them, but only a full surrender to God through faith in the Lord Jesus Christ."[6]

By the 1950's, James's reputation for preaching travelled before him. An English missionary wondered why someone like McKeown was having such an impact on the country. He decided to go along to a meeting one evening and joined the crowd of Africans pushing towards the centre of the town. Suddenly, children were shouting, "There's McKeown, there's the man!" An old fellow hobbling along with his traditional cloth draped over one shoulder exclaimed, "A fire burn in me when this man preach!"

As soon as James stood on a makeshift platform, the crowd quietened. He spoke in English, and every two sentences he would pause while a tall African to the right of him and a short one to the left translated his words into local dialects. Occasionally they stumbled, especially when James forgot to tone down his Scottish accent, but for the most part all three flowed together remarkably well, each one beginning to speak just before the last had finished.

James preached without notes, quoting the Bible chapter and verse from memory. First he used his imagination to paint a word-picture of the veil of the temple being torn in two. Then he started to ask his audience questions. "Everywhere I go in your country," he said, "in your shops and on your mammy lorries, I see the words *Gye Nyame.* What do they mean?"

"They mean – 'except God'," everyone shouted.

6 *Ibid.*

"Ah! You have it in your hearts to worship *Nyame,* the creator, the master of everything. Except for God, none of us would be here, would we? Nothing would exist. But *Nyame* is up high in the sky. How can you know him? How can you know that when you die you will live with him?" James paused and looked all round. "I tell you, God has made a way. Here in God's book it says, 'And this is life eternal, that they might know thee the only true God, *and Jesus Christ, whom thou hast sent.'* (John 17:3 AV – my italics)

Quietly and carefully, James went on to explain how how sacrificing animals to *Nyame* does not bring salvation. They could only come to know God through Jesus, who became the sacrifice to end all sacrifices. "And it was at the moment of his death that the veil of the Temple was torn in two. Do you know what that means?" asked James. "It means that we can enter the holiest place of God, if we put our trust in Jesus. All of us have done wrong. We deserve to die, but Jesus died instead of us. His blood breaks the power that sin has over us, so that we can become holy as He is holy. You see, salvation does not come through the blood of animals, but through the blood of Jesus. Some of you have Bibles in your own language. Go and look it up in Hebrews 10:4."

"Is there any other sacred purpose for which you use blood?" James asked. "In the ceremony for *enstooling* (enthroning) our chiefs," replied a lady, whose rich dress and huge gold ear-rings showed her to be a queen mother. "You use blood in the enthronement ceremony? You know, each one of us can be enstooled as chiefs in God's *Oman,* God's Kingdom! God is the *Omanhene,* the Paramount Chief of chiefs. The Bible says the blood of Jesus makes *us* kings and priests under God! Yes, priests as well, because we have free access to Him."

The crowd was so responsive, they began to ask James questions. This was not so much a sermon, more a dialogue. It was nothing like the sort of preaching the English missionary had been led to expect. He had seen crowds of

Africans transfixed by emotional preaching in the 'Spiritual' churches – and worried that their response was often ungodly in its intensity. But James was no fiery preacher. His words were slow and measured; he was calm and precise, never exciting his audience by human means. There was no clever oratory, just profound truth, expressed in a way the Africans could understand. James watched the crowd while his translators spoke. If some faces looked blank, he would ask more questions until they followed him. Once, he saw a section of the crowd had their attention distracted by some market traders. "I have noticed," he said, with a twinkle in his eye, "that African women are more intelligent than the men." At once both sexes were all ears, and eager to answer questions!

On other occasions throughout the sermon, James used a kind of catch-phrase. "Victory!" he declared, and some of his hearers shouted back, *"Through the blood of Jesus."* "Holiness..." *"Unto the Lord,"* "Christ in you..." *"The hope of glory!"*, or "If you don't go to heaven..." *"Don't blame Jesus"*.

At the end of the sermon, James asked any who wished to respond to the claims of Jesus to come to the front. As a result of his simple appeal, thirty men and women were told to face the congregation, with their hands raised in surrender to Jesus. They confessed that they had sinned and called upon the name of Jesus for salvation, then some Church leaders took them aside for counselling and prayer.

The missionary was amazed. He had never seen Africans respond in this way. How many times had he written out well-constructed sermons only to find that many in the congregation slept as he preached? After their hard day's work in the hot sun, he could hardly blame them, yet McKeown held everyone's attention. The man did not even have the benefit of a theological training!

"How could so quiet a man have such an impact?" the missionary asked a well-educated African standing next to him. The man thought for a moment, "You would not expect a brand new Mercedes to make much noise, but it has great power!" he replied. "You know what it is Pastor McKeown has that most leaders lack? Honesty and simplicity! We have no need of anything complicated, just someone to preach Jesus Christ crucified for our salvation. McKeown's preaching is backed by the power of the Holy Spirit. He uses no lofty words or human wisdom, yet we know his message comes from God. He directs people always towards Jesus and if you are sharing Christ with him, you cannot lose the way!"

"Are you in his Church?" asked the missionary. "Yes. My father was a Presbyterian minister, but I knew nothing of the power of God in my life until I heard Pastor McKeown. He was different. He was saying, 'Jesus is here'. Others preached, 'Jesus over there.' He told me about the Holy Spirit – through this I found the Lord *is* not *was.* Also, I could see Jesus in him. Other churches permitted sin even in pastors: McKeown preached holiness in the Church – he taught God could deliver you. I went to church before but it made very little difference in my life. Most of us churchgoers still followed our old pagan customs – but Pastor McKeown brought such a revelation of Jesus, we knew we should live differently from then on."

"I should like to meet this Pastor McKeown," said the missionary and before long he was shaking James's hand. "Tell me how you preach with such authority?" he asked.

James looked surprised, "Well, my friend, I do not think I preach very well. It would never do back in the UK! I have only three important messages – One: Jesus Christ and him crucified. Two: the Baptism of the Holy Spirit. Three: the power of God to change lives and bring holiness in the Church. I never use notes. I pray until the sermon is written on my heart and then my words bring conviction of sin and changed lives. You know, there are some who are afraid to come near our meetings in case the Spirit 'catches' them too!"

"Do many of your new converts fall away?" asked the missionary. "Very few," James replied. "Those who came forward today will be baptised within a month and we shall continue to teach them. Some of them cannot read, so we have to find ways of teaching them the Bible. You heard me shout a phrase and they responded. That is one way of helping people remember things.

"Then, when I feel I have a message from God for the Church, I do not preach that message just once. I might preach it at the general convention but then I go round all the regions preaching it again, to make sure the people have caught the meaning. And, each time after I have preached I will ask certain individuals if my words came across as they should, or if I could have done better.

"Sometimes we have what I call 'digging sessions' in the bush. I tell stories from the Bible. The Africans warm to this and we laugh together. They begin to feel relaxed with me and ask more questions. You know – this can be vital. My translators are very good, but misunderstandings do arise. Once, in the north, I was not getting the response I expected. I asked what my interpreter was saying, and was told, 'He's discussing how many cows you need to buy a wife!'"

James called a young man over. "Tell me, you were saved last month, were you not? Were you in church on Sunday? What did I preach? What were my points and how are you applying them in your life?" The young man impressed the missionary with his answers. "This is what I do whenever I meet people," explained James, "Encourage them to become not only hearers of the word, but doers also."

"But – is it always so easy?" asked the missionary. "No – people are not always ready to change. Look how there is a sameness about everything in the Gold Coast. We have the same length of day all the year round. Except for the rainy season, the weather knows little change. There is no change of fashion and no change of diet, everything goes on eternally the same. So we should not be surprised to find difficulties when new thought is introduced. These African villagers fear the effect of change. Still – though this work of ours can be hard and frustrating, it is not all sadness. One time I preached at Wassa Simpa on the text 'Buy the truth, and sell it not.' (Proverbs 23:23 AV) All the town were present, and when I returned at a later date, I was delighted that they came out to greet me with the words, 'Buy the truth, and sell it not, Pastor!'"

James went on to explain how, when people fell in love with Jesus, they would decide to form themselves into a local church. Elders would be appointed from among them and these, not James, baptised the new converts. Obviously, James could not stay in the place forever, though training new Christians, especially the leaders, was not accomplished over-night. His strategy was to hold central conventions for more evangelism and teaching. These larger gatherings were held in the open air. Canopies of palm branches held up by bamboo poles gave shade from the sun and concrete blocks borrowed from builders supported the planks used for benches – a very flexible system. "It wasn't all McKeown – we learnt it from the Methodists," James said. "The first convention I held was in 1939 in Winneba, when the whole Church, gathered together, numbered just 200."

The last general convention for the whole Church was in 1985 when 125,000 gathered in Accra. It brought the capital's traffic to a standstill. For obvious logistical reasons, general conventions have had to be replaced by regional ones such as we attended. Public address systems have been in use in the Church for years and mean open-air music and preaching can be heard over a wide area. Outsiders are drawn to the edge, curious, and Church members are appointed to look out for them and share the good news. The many conventions and rallies draw attention in a land where there are few other distractions or entertainments. They are like the Church's combine harvester, reaping thousands of souls every year.

Back in the early days, James once gave some toffees to a group of children and noticed they did not eat them all but took some back to their families and friends. He realised that, whenever someone gave away what they knew of Jesus, the good news would not stop there, but would be shared with all that person's circle of acquaintances. James claimed, with some truth, that he was never once responsible for opening a church. His role was, "To tell people the Bible way and set a fire burning in their hearts; then they went about setting flames here and there."

Eunice Addison said some remarkable words, "People think that because James does not perform anything spectacular he hasn't got power, but they don't know that the power really rests with this man in the spoken word. As the word comes out it breaks up and bears fruit in diverse colours. He told others, 'Here in the word you can prophesy,' or, ' You can go and heal.' All we see in the Church came by the word he faithfully stood and preached, together with his life. He laid down his life and the Lord resurrected him to preach that word faithfully."

Even in the capital there were totally pagan people, as well as many who knew something about Christianity. James preached in the open-air so as to catch people coming out of work. In 1947 he was preaching from the story of the Fall, where God asks Adam, "Where art thou?" (Genesis 3:9 AV) James changed this to, "Joseph, where art thou?", just as a man called Joseph Egyir Paintsil was walking by. This man had never seen James before, but his attention was caught. He was to become a great pastor, taking over the day-to-day leadership of the Church of Pentecost as James grew older. Pastor Paintsil had received a good education from the Methodists. He was not only highly intelligent and well-read, but he became a spiritual giant of a man who travelled all over West Africa and further afield as the Church's able ambassador.

Church growth was slow at first, with only a few women responding, but it only took men like Joseph Paintsil to be converted for growth to mushroom. Once saved, the Africans were passionate for the Gospel and preached from dawn to dusk. It is easier to evangelise in a climate where everyone stands around chatting in the open air. Pastor Safo explained, "Someone will just meet a friend in a market and a little testimony of Jesus works wonders. When a person says something about fetishes, you say 'No, but today I have seen Jesus.' 'How come?' 'He is in me' and the whole day that person would be following you to hear more." In West Africa it is common for people to migrate to new areas to find work and they would not stop evangelising. Sometimes people would even move especially, in order to be able to spread the good news to another part of the country.

God was on the move and sometimes people were converted without anyone preaching. Once, a driver was tired of waiting to take his passengers back from a big convention to their homes. Hearing them all praying, "Jesus, Jesus," he jeered at them, shouting, "Yes, Jesus, come quickly so I can get my passengers back soon to Cape Coast." Immediately this driver dropped to the ground under the power of God and had to be carried away. He became a Christian and later a prophet in the Church and was much used in healing.

Such dramatic conversions were not uncommon in a Church that had learned to pray. To give another example, there was once a young girl from a village up in the hills near Obo who sang for the fetish priest. When her brother was converted she asked, "Can there be any power greater than Tigare ?" (a pagan shrine). He told her to come to an Apostolic meeting and see but when she heard the Gospel, she was not convinced. On the way home she saw in the alley ahead of her a man, all covered in blood. "Who is this man and who has beaten him? Is there a murderer here?," she asked herself. The blood was pouring down from his head, but as she approached, the man turned his eyes. "I died for you," he said. Realising He was Jesus, she gave her life to Him and started going to the Apostolic Church.

When the girl was about 14, her father and then her brother died. The uncle who took her in was furious that she had joined James's Church and sent her miles away to Accra, to live with a woman who ran a chop (food) bar. There she had to lift a heavy eight-foot stick to pound fu-fu all day, but the woman gave her no wages or food.

Adabraka assembly had just opened nearby. This remarkable girl, far from feeling bitter, thought it was wonderful that God had given her somewhere to worship, although she was far from her church in Obo. Through all her hardships she was happy, because in the evening she could go and play her tambourine in the meeting. Though she had no food, she did not feel hungry. Then God told her to look in a corner and she found a pound note. She spent it wisely and when it was finished, God told her where to find another.

The girl's uncle arranged her marriage to a very short man he hoped would ill-treat her and prevent her going to church. Still, she prayed for this uncle who had been the cause of all her misfortunes. One day he arrived in Accra and, as soon as he came into the room, the Lord's hand touched him. In the evening the girl found him in church surrendering his heart to Jesus and later he became an elder in Accra West assembly.

God had given the girl a promise, "Because you have been faithful against all odds, alone, a little girl, you will never be sick. Your husband is so short, but I will give you children that are nice to look at." Both promises have come to pass and her own relatives say, "If it were not for the Lord we would say these are not our uncle's children."

The Witness Movement helped mobilise the young Church for evangelism. It was started in the late 1940's by Pastor Stanley Hammond, an Apostolic missionary working with James. It's aim was to train young people to win the country for Christ, but the older people refused to be excluded!

Within this movement sprang up the even more radical 'Bombing Group', led by a young electrician named Johnny Mallet. Just after the war, twelve young people in Accra decided to go and 'bomb' the enemy through evangelism. This group was responsible for starting most of the assemblies in Greater Accra. Each Friday, after work, they would go and evangelise. At first they had no transport, but Johnny had promotion at work and with it a firm's car. Every weekend, they would drive as far as the northern Volta Region, ten of them in his Morris Minor. Johnny grinned at my expression of disbelief, "I've been to Lomé – the capital of Togo!" he told me. "When our number increased, the Lord gave me another car, bigger size. Oh, hallelujah!"

They would not set out until God had spoken through prophecy as to where they should go and there they would spend the weekend, preaching in the open air until Sunday night. The group then reported back to Accra – "There are twenty converts in this place – please send someone to be in charge". This proved a headache for the Church because in those days there were not many full-time pastors. James, though, saw that these young people, so passionate for the Gospel, were the leaders of the future. Without them, he could never realise his goal of confronting every soul in the country with the Word: with them, whole tracts of Africa might be reached. He took a special interest in them – helping, encouraging, teaching, discipling. From that tiny group have emerged three apostles, as well as prominent pastors, elders and deaconesses.

There is a single-mindedness about these Ghanaian

Christians. They are dedicated to evangelism. Issues of good and evil are clear-cut and the essential Gospel truth is not fudged by the distractions of materialism. Evangelism is the priority and this fact shapes the Church. Though they preach excellent Gospel messages, there is little time for complex Bible teaching – but then Jesus's first disciples did not need degrees in theology to change the world.

Eunice Addison said, "How great is our God James brought! What he spoke on that first day is still working. When James preached, he said his word would bear fruit and that they would stand amazed. It has borne all this in Ghana – and even greater things can the Lord do. James came to preach Jesus Christ and not himself and since he is no longer here, we have Christ in our midst." By making evangelism the top priority, by simple, anointed preaching which communicated to the hearers on their ground and by mobilising others in spreading the good news, James made a way for the Spirit of God to move and grow the Church.

# Chapter 8
# The Clash of Two Kingdoms

The Church reached the capital, Accra, in 1944. An African radio fitter called A. S. Mallet travelled to Cape Coast to hear James speak. As a result, he was filled with the Spirit and asked James to visit the group of nine new believers he led in Accra. The third time James came to the group, they begged for a permanent pastor. J. A. C. Anaman was sent and in a year, numbers had reached 100.

Up to this time, the Church had consisted of just a few low-profile assemblies in Central and Western Region. Then, in 1945, they held an Easter convention in an area of Accra which rejoices in the name of 'Merry Villas'. This convention proved to be a turning point. Miracles which happened there drew the attention of the press and were reported all over the country. Now James was invited to other small groups who wanted to hear about the Holy Spirit, and more opportunities opened for him and his co-workers to travel and share the Gospel.

Johnny Mallet joined the Church in Accra, at a time when it consisted of just twenty-five believers. People came peeping through the windows, laughing and throwing stones. James's Church was considered mad because no-one else worshipped as they did. At the time no other church allowed clapping in meetings. If heard, they could be fined, because there were specific times when clapping was prohibited in the country's traditional religion – it was said to disturb the spirits. The group in Accra, crammed into a private house, were forced to shut the windows, despite the heat.

The group met right over to one side of the city, so young Johnny decided to start a new assembly in a suburb on the other side. For two and a half years he walked the five miles from his home to Labadi, carrying his lamp and accordion.

The fetish priests and priestesses became so agitated about the clapping in Johnny's Labadi services that one day all of them invaded the little meeting, throwing stones and beating the people with brooms. There was such a commotion that the British police, for the sake of peace, asked the church not to return to Labadi. "But God brought us back, and see it today!" smiled Johnny, pointing to the huge Labadi church building, which seats 5,000.

Around 45% of the population still follow Ghana's traditional religion – animism. The supreme being is a remote sky god who deals with the world through various intermediaries – minor gods who might live in stones, rivers or household objects. An inanimate object, worshipped because it is the dwelling place of a spirit or has magical powers, is known as a 'fetish' and its priests as 'fetish priests'. These priests influence events or foretell the future. Dead ancestors also have power over living people. One person can bring calamity on another by influencing the gods or ancestors through witchcraft or 'ju-ju'. Ordinary people spend vast sums on charms or amulets to protect them from these things because fear and real evil grip most people's lives. As one of James's pioneer pastors put it, "You have your cultural practices. Ours tend to lead us into worship of fetishes – into all kinds of sin and diabolical spiritism. This dominated us and our way of life."

'Diabolical spiritism' has never been hidden in Ghana as it is in the UK. As James travelled along the roads, he noticed a white piece of cloth flying from a stick at the entrance to many villages. He was told it was a sign that the local fetish priest or priestess was available for consultation. He loved to watch the women carrying their babies tied onto their backs with a piece of the same material used for their beautiful dresses. Then James realised some of the 'babies' were dolls. Some women who were having trouble conceiving believed that carrying dolls would work sympathetic magic to give them real babies. These things are still practised today.

In 1939 James wrote, "On one occasion I entered a home on a pastoral visit. The first person I met was the head of the home, in his arms he was carrying a new-born baby. I looked at the lovely little face and saw three incisions in its forehead with a certain medicine rubbed on them. I asked how the baby had received such injuries, but was told that the baby had not been injured, but as there were certain relatives in the family who possessed evil spirits, the parents, by making these incisions and applying the medicine, had protected the child from (their) influence."

"It is common to hear the beating of drums and other strange noises, and on reaching the spot one will find many people gathered, sitting in the form of a ring, and in the ring a few will be dancing to the beat of drums. The dance is usually led by a woman who is supposed to be under the power of the spirit or spirits; she prophesies to them and tells them what to do in order to evoke the spirit's power. Such a company is in no way graceful to behold, as most of them may be well under the influence of strong drink and the leading woman partially nude... The soothsayer or diviner may tell them to bring a sheep or goat, or sometimes a good sum of money. It may also be revealed that someone is causing the trouble, in return they get some medicine in which is supposed to be the spirit's power and which will keep away sickness or other evil spirits. This medicine is taken home and placed in the house or about it somewhere."[1]

The stage was set for a very real battle between the kingdom of darkness and the Kingdom of light, but when James was first at work, most Christian missions in the area did not see it that way. They neglected evangelism at a time when new pagan cults were springing up. In the 1920s and 30s, research by anthropologists influenced the British colonial government to preserve African traditional religion.

1 Pastor James McKeown, "African Beliefs and Practices in the Gold Coast", *Herald of Grace* (1939) p 124.

Into this environment were born cults such as Tigare which became so popular, people left the churches in droves to join them. These so-called anti-witchcraft shrines claimed anyone who did not join them was a witch. While they quoted from the Bible – you shall not fornicate or kill – they gave no power for changed lives. So when someone broke a commandment, the priests of these shrines demanded a huge fine – or threatened death. Many Christians joined: James's Church stood out against the shrines and helped turn the tide in the religious history of the country.

Given this environment of demonic activity, it was just as well James was used to dealing with such things. Back in his Glasgow church, Andrew Turnbull was renowned for the direct and authoritative way he dealt with demonised people. Similarly, the Church in Ghana has learnt the power of the Cross over demons. It is rare for someone not to have been involved with spirit worship before becoming a Christian. Prayer at conversion to cut off past influences is vital and fetish objects are destroyed as soon as is practically possible.

The Church takes involvement in pagan practices so seriously that any member who remains involved is suspended from membership and demoted from any Church office they held. Other churches often turn a blind eye to such things, or even incorporate elements of pagan religion into their worship. Pagan worshippers often enter a trance-like state in which they are able to do super-human things. If anything remotely like that ever occurs in a Church of Pentecost meeting, the leaders deal with it at once.

Pressure on Church members to pour libations to the gods at funerals or tribal festivals is often intense. A chief in Ghana still has power and can order that no-one goes to farm, or drums on certain days so as not to disturb the spirits. Christians can suffer persecution or go before a court over these things, but if the Kingdom of light is to stay in the light, it cannot let the darkness in.

Persecution began right back in the late 1930s when three

friends of James's were imprisoned because they refused to perform certain fetish rites demanded by their chief. One was S. R. Asomaning, and another was James Gyimah, the first man to be filled with the Spirit in the Gold Coast. When they were imprisoned, the rest of the Church prayed and the results were dramatic. The next day the chief mysteriously vanished, the men were released and the local people took note, because although the chief was found again, from that day on he lived a miserable existence. In the end persecution often seemed to help the spread of the Gospel.

Church buildings were burnt to the ground. Once someone threw a dead cat at James and it was common for preachers to be stoned in the street – yet God protected his people from serious injury. Still, the Church was never content with defensive action against Satan: they were always on the attack. Many in the Brong Ahafo region had never heard of Jesus until Pastor Owusu with a few others trekked right out into the bush. They walked an average of 25 miles a day, fording rivers, and when they reached a village, would expect some people to be saved and filled with the Spirit. Others would come and curse the evangelists. This was a serious thing, but Owusu and his friends found that they could withstand even the witch-doctors in the name of Jesus, and that the power of evil could be turned around. Jesus's power was demonstrated when the lame walked and the blind saw. The ju-ju men had been trying to chase the evangelists away but instead, Owusu turned round and started chasing them, preaching the Gospel all the time. Many turned to Christ.

One pastor talked about evangelism in the 1940s: "We went out to preach the Gospel in the villages around Suhum – but we did not know where our enemies were. So we never went out except by the power and promises of Jesus – until we had assurance in our hearts of his protection. Then we went to the villages and challenged them to try to hurt us through ju-ju. They would do their best to destroy us. Then, when nothing happened, the people in the village were convinced Jesus was the most powerful and they converted. You see, it was not just the appearance of Christianity – people saw the power of the Holy Spirit. Fetish spirits also prophesy and do certain things, but when we prayed, the Holy Spirit overpowered these spirits. This made people marvel – that there was a greater power than their fetishes. People found Jesus brought deliverance from evil spirits and that he gave real protection against witchcraft, so they destroyed their ju-ju."

More recently, the Church held a Witness Movement rally in a town where a fetish priestesses' convention was also taking place. Aware of the evil around, the Church was praying hard, but one evening, the priestesses roasted unripe pawpaw until they were red hot and catapulted them into the crowd of young Witnesses. Miraculously, not one person was hit, but this Church was not content with a passive victory. The leader had all the missiles brought to the front of the meeting where they were counted. There were 120. "We claim one soul for every pawpaw thrown," he declared – and 120 people were saved that night.

Another time, three major churches in one town were closed down by a witch-doctor. Next, he went at night to try to kill one of James's pastors but twice a wall of fire prevented him. The third time an angel gave him a blow which left him blind and paralysed. The man sent for the pastor he had tried to kill and asked for prayer. Immediately, the demons and witchcraft were defeated; the man was healed, saved and ready to begin a new life of service for God.

Direct confrontation also came from a man called Gakpo, a much-feared Ewe witch-doctor. (Voodoo originated with the Ewe tribe and was exported to the Caribbean via the slave trade.) At Accra Convention we heard this huge man tell how he tried for years to kill Pastor McKeown. In 1946 he had seen James and some of the other Pastors singing, 'Let Your mighty power' at a meeting and Gakpo realised these people had a life and power such as he had not seen in a church before. He was furious and started throwing stones. Being almost seven feet tall and powerfully built, Gakpo was used to others cowering before his sheer physical presence. When every stone missed its target he was surprised. When A. S. Mallet came up and prophesied that one day God would touch him and then catch him, Gakpo was affronted.

Next, Gakpo turned his ju-ju against the pastors, but they were unharmed. He enlisted the help of an even more powerful witch-doctor and together they made a medicine which not only had magic qualities but was poisonous too. This they put in James's bread and watched by their occult powers in a mirror to see when he would die. As James ate the bread, they saw another man with him. That man broke the mirror and no harm came to James.

Gakpo realised there was a very strong power in James, and the desire to kill him became an obsession. He followed James from town to town, trying everything he knew, but to no avail. At one convention, Gakpo's magic caused it to rain, but the pastors prayed. Though it continued pouring all around, over the canopy it was dry. Gakpo had to acknowledge these people were stronger than he. Back home, Gakpo called on his ju-ju, but they would not work again and his whole body became very cold. He remembered A. S. Mallet's prophecy that God would touch him. At last he surrendered himself to God. The day he was baptised, many of his ju-ju friends became Christians and later he went with James round the Volta region, where Voodoo holds sway, testifying to the power of Jesus.

Ghana is a place where witchcraft and demon worship are practised openly, yet, despite this, large parts of the country are free from a feeling of oppressive evil. There is a battle in heavenly places and the Church is used to seeing victory. It seems as though they have turned the spiritual atmosphere through prayer and this is one reason that people are free to respond to the Gospel in the way they do.

The clash of two kingdoms was never evenly matched. Satan can only counterfeit, but the Holy Spirit demonstrates in reality and power. This was why the Church found the gifts, fruits and ministry of the Holy Spirit were vital in evangelism. Before James, only the American Assemblies of God missionaries had preached the Baptism of the Holy Spirit, but their following was small. According to James, not only did the Americans find it hard to overcome in-bred colour prejudice, but they were so rich and highly educated, they seemed to the Africans to be from another planet.

H. W. Debrunner, who wrote the standard *History of Christianity in Ghana*[2] said churches there were predominantly middle class, a society set apart. Ordinary people were looking for emotional experience, healing and security from devils as well as for social fellowship. The churches were only providing the last: the fetish cults claimed to provide all four. Then James came preaching the full Gospel which could be seen to work better than the fetish cults and that was why so many flocked to his church. The Holy Spirit made Jesus real to people and helped them know him in their hearts as well as in their heads. Christianity was no longer a matter of intellectual assent: through the Holy Spirit people knew that "Jesus *is* not Jesus *was*."

Most churches taught that the gifts of the Holy Spirit were only for Bible times. Some Africans had read how Jesus and the early disciples delivered the demonised and healed the sick, but it seemed no more than a nice old story. Now, in James's Church, they actually saw it happening. The cripples were walking, the blind seeing and even, in some cases, the dead rising. Many were convinced of the living truth of the Bible and decided to follow Jesus for the first time. Others left their old churches because they were thirsty for this 'new thing' being proclaimed and demonstrated.

2 Hans W Debrunner, *op cit.*

There were three kinds of churches, according to James. He labelled them as spiritual, demonic and commonsense. A spiritual church "Is where the doors of the hearts of the members are open to the Holy Spirit and his manifestations. Evil spirits seeking entrance are detested." In a demonic church, on the other hand, *any* spiritual influence is allowed to dominate. "People in this church can prophesy and speak in tongues as did King Saul, though he was filled with greed, position-seeking and intentions to kill David for earthly gain. We should take heed that evil influences do not come into the Ghana Apostolic Church lest it turn out to be the worst sect in Africa. Striving for holiness and truth is a sure sign that there are those filled with the Holy Spirit. A commonsense church is one which, because of confusion, has closed its doors to anything supernatural. They worship God in the realm of acquired commonsense to the commendation of a commonsense society. Jesus came to build a spiritual, holy Church. We want to be such a church in Ghana." [3]

At first, the gifts of the Holy Spirit were so unfamiliar, there were many misunderstandings. One lady spoke in tongues and then was afraid to go to sleep in case she 'lost' the gift. People went to the bush to receive the Holy Spirit during long 'tarrying meetings'. One young man could not see why this was necessary. He shut himself in his room and waited on God. When he emerged hours later, full of the Spirit, he found a crowd around his door. They were worried and thought he had died. He was able to tell them, not only was he more alive than ever before, but he had met with God in a very special way. He went on to become a powerful evangelist and an apostle in the Church.

When people who had been dominated by evil spirits were freed by Jesus and filled with the Holy Spirit, there was no holding them back. One former fetish priestess was so

3 James speaking as recorded in 1961 Council minutes of the Church of Pentecost.

vigourous when she danced in praise of Jesus that they had to clear a large area. She was 75, and James wondered if it were not too much for her. She replied, "For years I danced before the Devil – now I'm going to expend my energy dancing before Jesus!"

From the mid-40s on, the Church's growth was by multiplication rather than addition. Because Jesus was so real in the experience of the new Christians, because they experienced deliverance from demons and being filled with the Holy Spirit, the change in their lives was evident to all who knew them. Sometimes there were dramatic changes – many drunkards found God enabled them to give up alcohol. But the new found joy of all the converts, together with their concern for others, drew people to the Church.

A tree grows slowly at first, but once its root system and a few branches are established, there is no holding it and soon seeds are being carried far and wide. A few people heard James's words of faith. They were set on fire for Jesus, equipped with the power of the Holy Spirit and totally committed to spreading the Gospel. They could testify to the power of God over all that Satan could hurl against them and they knew the power of the Holy Spirit to change lives. They attacked the forces of darkness and won. Village by village, area by area, the Gold Coast was succumbing to the Gospel. Soon it would be spilling out across Africa.

# Chapter 9
# A People Pure and Holy

In all the meetings we attended in Ghana, we listened to millions of words in strange languages, yet one word, the first I ever learnt in Twi, stood out. It was *kron kron* which means 'holy'. When the sermons were translated, we found a constant theme was how each Christian should submit to God's control and live in a way which pleased Him.

When James lived in Cape Coast there was an Anglican school just below his house and James learnt lessons from watching the young Ghanaian students there. They seemed to have little interest in God and James did not like some of the things he saw going on. He realised that many who called themselves Christians in the Gold Coast were seen as hypocrites, who preached one thing and practised another. The only difference Jesus made to their lives was that they went to church. This was hardly a good advertisement for the Gospel, because, if Jesus was all He claimed to be, He gave His disciples power for a much more radical change.

From the beginning, James always went back to the Cross where Jesus died in order to save people not only from Satan, but from their sins. He said, "Other missionaries came to teach sewing and did not get down to the root of the problem. It is only the Cross that will spoil sin. Nothing else will." If people said they had accepted Jesus but continued to want to do wrong, the darkness would engulf them. In other words, there is a clash of two kingdoms, but living in the Kingdom of light is not just about keeping clear of demonic activity. James knew that unless the Church was pure, drawing its nourishment only from Jesus, it would never grow. He looked not for excitement and emotion in response to the Gospel, but for changed lives.

There were many tribes in the Gold Coast. Each person

owed allegiance to the paramount chief of an *oman* – a tribal kingdom or nation within the country. James taught Jesus was the Chief of chiefs and his church was to be *oman kron kron* – a holy nation set apart from the rest of society, not because they wore different clothes or went to church on Sunday, but because their whole lives were under God's rule.

James found that people were often happy to accept the good news about Jesus but wanted to keep their old ways as well. Nackabah's Church was a good example. There appeared to be a great response to the Gospel but then, over the issue of 'one man, one wife', the majority were lost. After all he had gone through in the village, this must have been painful for James but he would never compromise. If people were not prepared to accept Jesus as Lord, he did not want them in the Church.

Polygamy was not the only problem. Lies were a way of life, sex outside of marriage was not considered to be wrong, the abuse of alcohol was common and money was often a stumbling block. James said the people did not become saints overnight. He had to educate, train and disciple – and he had to be ruthless in cutting off any evil from the Church.

The first way James taught was by the example of his own life. The Africans would never have accepted all the discipline had they seen any hypocrisy in him. More than that, James restored their faith in the fact Jesus could deliver a person from sin. Because James was a man of integrity who stood by what he said, they themselves were encouraged to take a stand. Pastor Safo perhaps paid James the greatest compliment of all when he explained, "They say I am like James. This is because I happen to be trying to live the life I see in him."

It is easy to think of missionary pioneers as a breed apart, but they are not exempt from temptation. In 1939, James wrote that, "Character is essential where the air is charged with demons and the atmosphere thick with sensuality." The drumming and dancing, which were so much part of village life, had strong sexual, as well as demonic connotations. When James stayed in a remote village without his wife, it was not unknown for mothers to offer to sell their daughters to him for the duration of his visit. Even if the approach was not so blatant, he could not fail to notice the many opportunities to go astray. "I was born a man and not an angel!" he said, "But if crows drop their dirt on you, it's up to you to clean it off. I was tempted, but, by the grace of God, I was always able to keep from sin. There were times when I nearly lost my temper and flattened somebody with my fist – but you have to do things God's way."

Another area in which James had to guard his spirit was that of pride. He said the Africans love to flatter, but the Holy Spirit flatters no-one and it was important not to have a swelled head. He also came to the conclusion that shyness was a form of pride and struggled to overcome his natural reticence. "The root of sin is 'I' ", he said, "We have to take Jesus's yoke upon us and learn of Him. The secret of success in ministry is to take up the Cross and deny yourself." The Ghanaians found James to be selfless – always prepared to make sacrifices in order to help others.

As well as setting a good example, James laid out various clear guidelines which applied to the culture of the country. Men should have legal (as distinct from customary) marriages, limiting them to one wife and making divorce difficult to obtain. The Akan people make up a good part of the population of Ghana. Akan society is matrilineal which means the inheritance goes to the men through the mother's side – normally to the mother's sister's children. The nephews inherit, not the sons – which causes all sorts of problems, especially in cases of intermarriage between tribes. James taught that sons should inherit, which the parents could arrange by making proper wills. Tribalism was not to be permitted in the Church; there should not be separate assemblies for different tribes in any location, even if this meant language difficulties. Alcohol was a curse in the country and Church members were expected to abstain. Sometimes, James could sound legalistic, but he looked in faith to Jesus to work in those who were true disciples. He once said, "Polygamists and liars are not to be driven from the Church in the literal sense. The Word of God, if well applied, will set members of the Church in order, or make those unfit leave by themselves."

In the early days, the Church spent so much time in prayer that, when they met together, the presence of God was there in a powerful way. James said, "If we are truly in the presence of God, no liar can stay there." There was a real sense of the fear of God. Everyone knew the Holy Spirit would reveal sin. People only dared try to join the Church if they had good intentions. Sometimes non-Christians would come along even when no-one had brought them, weeping and confessing their sin.

Once a woman had stolen some fish and the same day was in Church singing praise to God. The Holy Spirit spoke to the lady sitting next to her and that word became fire in the thief's bones. She could not sit still, but went to confess to the elders while they were taking the collection.

In many ways, sin in the Church was more difficult to deal with than was blatant confrontation with demonic powers. James normally faced issues head-on and could be devastatingly clear and honest where sin was involved. He was a man of few, but powerful words. The Africans grew to appreciate James for being straight-forward and always speaking his mind. They knew where they were with him and that they would not get away with anything, because he would always bring things out into the open.

James admitted, "I was not a nice missionary." Once he worked with a missionary who was so nice that he could see no evil in anybody. James said if he had been like that it would have spelt disaster for the Church. "You need to know where you are as a missionary and not be easily disturbed, even if it means conflict. Principle is the principal thing."

If he sensed something was wrong, James would not rest until it was put right and he could be so preoccupied that friends would say, "James, you passed me and never spoke." If the culprits would not confess their sin, often he would have such a specific word of knowledge from God, that they could no longer deny it. The Ghanaians told us, "Time and time again, James would arrive at a meeting and the Lord would show him things. We would have to wait on God till we were purged clean. Only then could we conduct the business, not before!"

During one of James's last visits to Ghana, he went to a meeting where the song leader had what he described as "more perspiration than inspiration." James sensed what was wrong and asked the man how old he was. "Twenty-six? Then it's time you were married!" The man said loftily that he had a higher calling than marriage. But after James made the twenty mile journey back home, he found two letters saying what a rascal this fellow had been with women. Straight away James sacked him from the platform. He chuckled, "I was not always a quiet man!"

At other times, James sensed what was wrong and, like the African he had become, told a story or proverb. The culprit would catch his meaning and go and put things right. James could be subtle and, occasionally, rather than wading into a situation with all guns blazing, he gave the person their head until it was obvious to everyone that they were being foolish. He was a good judge of character. He would often say of someone, "I liked him" or "I didn't trust her" and he was usually right. He learned to know people after the spirit and not after the flesh.

James made enemies, people left, yet most continued to follow him and the Church grew. They came to realise that he had no favourites – that no matter who misappropriated money or fell into immorality, instant judgement would come. One of the pastors explained, "When you commit any of these things and you hear James is coming, you leave your station before he comes, because it is not a matter of saying you are sorry and he will understand you. You have by all means to be disgraced and sent home." Not only that, James would ask, "Who brought this man into the ministry?" Church leaders are dismissed every so often, for some sin, or even for inefficiency, but, because of the strict standards set, it is a very small proportion of Church officers who need to be disciplined. Johnny Mallet said, "James impressed upon us that God will not use anybody who does not conform to the Word. If you speak nicely to the people and you yourself do not live in the Word, your word will become dead." In character as well as gift, James looked for an exceptionally high quality of leadership and this has made all the difference to Church growth.

Some feared James, yet as they got to know him better, they grew to love him, because he would stand by them. Johnny Mallet said, "When I did anything wrong, he used to pull my ears. He insisted on a clean life and truthfulness. James was very strict and hated sin but if anything troubled you – however bad – you could go and tell him. We are all human beings, all struggling one way or another. We all fall by the wayside and no-one lives without temptation – but if you told him what happened to you, he would pray for you and bring Scripture to support you and lift you up. He would teach you but he would never divulge any secret to anyone, that is why people at times ran to him. But when you told him lies and he found it out – then it was your own fault!"

Some things James had to deal with were more in the realm of training than sin. "Remember," he said, "much of the time I was not dealing with nice, well educated people, but with the nitty gritty of life, out in the bush." Ghanaians generally hate being out in the rain. One day, James arrived in a certain village tired. He took a bath, had a cup of tea and went to the hall to lead the evening meeting as arranged. Hardly a soul was there. When James asked why, he was told, "Pastor, it rain small, it is cold small, the people have gone to bed!" James caught hold of a four gallon kerosene tin and began to beat it with a stick. He set off to walk right through the village like this. The few who were with him laughed and did the same. Everyone came out to see what all the noise was about and soon they had their meeting. "I was known for this kind of thing in Ghana," chuckled James. "I was not a nice missionary and I did not learn it in Bible school!"

Another time, people were late to a meeting, so, when they did arrive, James picked up his Bible, called Sophia and went home. The next night he could hear a packed church singing, long before he reached the building. They were never late again! Then he found some Africans liked to sit near the window in meetings, so they could spit. "I'll tell them in England that you do this," threatened James and they were worried, "Please Pastor, we won't do it again!"

The women did not always keep silence in church. James said they would chatter away about all the details of childbirth and it was quite an education to him, because in those days, women back home never mentioned such things. When he made it clear they had not come to church to learn about after-births but about Jesus, the women paid attention.

A man's dignity is very important in Africa and to lose face or be rebuked in public is one of the worst things that can happen to him. There is a natural tendency to 'sweep things under the carpet.' Sometimes the cry would be, "Don't tell James!" yet James cut right across that.

Direct and used to authority, but never domineering, James had a tremendous presence about him, even if he said nothing. When he spoke, it was normally very quietly, but his words had a tremendous weight and power, as well as containing a wealth of wisdom. Even so, given the African's reluctance to lose face, how did they came to accept the authority of this white man? Someone explained, "James was our daddy and he could do things no-one else could," but had they not recognised where his authority came from, no-one would have followed him. People recognised that he had the mind of the Spirit.

James was always the master of any situation. Just as an African family would look to its head for direction, everyone looked to him. But it was not all James. Another reason the Africans accepted his authority was that he never tried to keep it to himself. From the beginning, James always involved the African leaders. Later he brought in an African executive to lead the Church and bring judgement where necessary, so that it was never a one-man-show.

Today, if someone is involved in immorality, cultic practices or cheating with money, it is announced publicly in the assemblies and that person is barred from taking Communion for a stated period. If at the end of that time they show the fruits of repentance, they are re-instated to membership, though not necessarily to office. Young members of the Witness Movement are very proud of their badges. If they fail to live up to the accepted moral standard, they have to give up the badge, even though they have paid for it. Many are wary of joining the Church of Pentecost in the first place, because the strictness of Church discipline is well known. This would seem to make the rate of Church growth all the more remarkable, but really it shows that continued growth is only possible because the foundation remains firm. Because converts make a complete break with the past, the drop-out rate is very low.

The order which is maintained in the Church of Pentecost's huge meetings would never be possible without Church discipline, nor would all their complex organisation in a society which tends towards the chaotic. For example, at the end of an Accra convention, the leader announced they wanted all the benches cleared. In the space of ten minutes, seating for 18,000 was neatly stacked by the road! Again, the Church's well-equipped vehicle maintenance workshop is almost unique in a country whose equivalent of our 'MOT' only requires one part of a vehicle to work – the horn! A more typical garage consists of a few bald tyres for sale, some rusting bits of iron and a notice proclaiming its excellence at repairing all known makes of transport!

Holiness is more than freedom from sin or obedience to a set of rules. People become more like God in character. In James's Church people show a love for one another and a care for the needy. If outsiders were impressed when bad people changed, they were even more impressed when they saw love in action.

Mrs Siriboe is the headmistress of a well-known school in Accra. It took something for her to join the Church. Coming from a wealthy family, she travelled abroad, had fine clothes, a car and a very good job as a mass-education officer. She was posted to Kumasi and happened to lodge with Church members. "They were so sweet a couple – even though I went into their house as a tenant, I was treated as a child. They would wait up if I was in late, to see I had something hot to eat. Once, I left a candle burning in my room and it set the place on fire, but to my amazement, I was not told off like I would have been at home. They had such love. I had not seen it in my family. I did not have it in me. This melted my heart and I asked my landlady, 'Mama, a sweet woman like you with your background, why do you go about clapping your hands with those people?' She said, 'Come and see.'

"I went to the meeting, just to observe, I would not go in properly, but sat right at the back. Then I saw a woman arriving very late. How she was running up the hill in all the heat! I sat there with my perfumes and fine clothes and this woman, perspiring heavily and smelling of fish, said please to push along so she could sit down. They were praying for the Holy Spirit, but I was just longing for it all to finish, when all of a sudden, the fish-wife was on the ground, sobbing, then beaming with joy and pouring out tongues. She did not know me, nor did the twelve year old at the other side who interpreted her tongue, but the message was all mine. It said all I had been doing and prophesied what I would be doing in the future, which has all come to pass since. All the bangles on my arm came off and my ear-rings. I knew I would not be the same again."

The fruits of the Spirit were growing on the tree that was the Church. They spread from branch to branch, containing the seeds of new growth within. James had sown the first seed and dug deep. The tree was nourished from the pure water of Jesus and not from any polluted source. Ask the Ghanaians what was James's main achievement, and you are told, "James's ministry changed lives. If you want to see the fruit of his labour, look around – it is us!"

# Chapter 10
# Equipping for Leadership

Any chronological account of James's life would be difficult to follow. After his first few years of ministry in the Gold Coast, James's life consisted of travelling around, preaching and visiting the numerous churches all over the country. By now the Church had spread so wide, it was easier for its head to live in the capital, where communications were centred. James made his final change of base in 1948, when he and Sophia moved from Cape Coast to Accra. At first they had a bungalow in an area called Adabraka, but later the Church built them a fine house to the east of Accra in Labadi. James said they often used to find snakes there, but he and Sophia were never bitten. This same building now forms part of the impressive Head Office of the Church of Pentecost.

James devoted himself to training his people. He saw this as a priority. James was quick to recognise gifts and to promote others. Once he had given people an appreciation of who God was and of who they were in God, James would get alongside them and train them. In Accra, he would set up a PA system during the day. When it was time for work to finish, his Africans lay preachers used it. James cleared it up himself when they had finished. People said of James, "He is not a gentleman, he works!" – but this was an efficient way of training his speakers and leaders. He especially took the keen young evangelists from the Bombing Group under his wing. One of them, Pastor L. A. Nyarko, said, "Sometimes James would give us a text to preach on and if you had not premeditated on it you would be terrified, but you had been called, so you had to do what you could. Later James would tell you what you should and should not have said. For example, originally we thought we were the best, so we would preach openly against all the other churches. That was one of our mistakes, but James found it out and told us "Don't mention the names of churches when preaching – just preach Jesus!"

Pastor Nyarko continued, "It was a very practical 'Bible school' and we learnt a great deal from James. He would take us to a place in Korle Bu where there were mango trees and every Tuesday evening, from seven to nine, he would teach us from Scripture. On Friday evenings we would pray, pray, pray and then he would teach us how to evangelise, how to preach as young men and women, how to communicate with others so we didn't cause any offence. That built us up and gave us a good and sound foundation. We were very privileged to be under his feet, teaching us and grooming us for the ministry. We were used in a lot of assignments in the Church, preaching in this and that assembly, opening up the work here and there and eventually we were made elders in charge of the assemblies we had established around Accra.

"James had a higher vision than our men. Sometimes we had trouble with our senior pastors when we went off at weekends to evangelise in Johnny's car. They told us not to be absent Sunday mornings because we all had served as song leaders etc in our local assemblies and we left a vacuum. But we did not wish just to sit in one place. James took our side, because he knew he himself could not open assemblies – he needed younger men to work with him. That, I think, was the main achievement of his life – he preached the Word and trained us to do the work."

This group of young people learnt from James. Its leader, Johnny Mallet, said, "I used to be very inquisitive. I wanted to know more about Jesus and James was very good to me, he took me on and taught me. He would encourage people. If I preached he would ask me to come and see him in his house and give me some lesson to study."

Prayer was emphasised. These young people spent hours waiting on God, alone or together, but James surprised them. They thought prayer was asking God things. James taught them to wait on God on their knees – and it might be a couple of hours before God spoke. At first they found this hard to cope with – until they realised that they did not have much success when they went out to preach, unless God had specified exactly where they were to go. Once this had happened James would lay hands on them and, in just a few words, ask the Lord to anoint them. As they went out, they found they had a fresh touch from the Holy Spirit.

James also taught them a love of the Bible and how to get themselves equipped from Scripture, so they could understand what they were doing. In one way, James was very simple. He just took the Bible and believed it and these young men had no problem doing the same.

From that small group, Apostles Paintsil, Hushie and Nartey rose to be among the highest leaders in the Church. Other pastors were Sackey, Vanderpuije, and L. A. Nyarko – all of whom had very significant ministries. In addition, Adotey and Diabah were founder members of the Bombing Group who later became leaders in other churches. Most of the other men and women in the group had an important role of their own to play as prominent elders, deaconesses etc.

James was their example as well as their teacher. Not only would he invest his ministry in them, but he would impart something of himself. Those he had been close to – they have his spirit about them – the same mixture of humility and authority, the same quiet but powerful wisdom, the same shining love of God, the same refusal to compromise.

When James first set out for Africa, did he have any idea of how he would organise any church that might emerge – or did he just preach the Gospel and wait to see what happened? James explained, "If you knew me, I'm very original. I think my own thoughts. I had in my mind two contrasting pictures from the farms back home in Ireland. The first was of my father, who was a good, hard-working man; on our farm he did everything himself. His children had to do this and that, but he planned, he ploughed, he decided what he wanted planted in each field and he didn't consult us children. I don't know if he intended it, but the effect was to keep us down and make us feel inferior. When my father retired, we children felt we could not rise to be farmers ourselves and, because none of us would take on the farm, it was sold.

"Then, I thought of some of our farming neighbours. If they were doing anything on the land, they consulted their children and all worked happily together. They grew up together as a family, loving one another, taking decisions together and learning to share the responsibility. The younger generation eventually bought other farms round about, and when their father grew old he didn't have to sell his farm. He could relax and leave it in the competent hands of his children.

"So, when I preached in Africa and people came to know the Lord, I engaged them to do the work. This was the reason the Church grew. I thought, 'If the Ghanaian women can do a job, why should I do it?' I taught them about finance and they released me from that burden. It was rare for me to baptise new converts, the Ghanaians did it. Tell me, who runs the Salvation Army in Ghana? Europeans. Who runs the Church of Pentecost? Ghanaians. You talk about my founding this Church but I could have never done all that. The Africans did it."

James never forced his leadership on anyone, but waited until he was invited to come and help. Soon the invitations were more than a few men could handle, so he had to look to God for more men of vision and ability. Quite early on, James wrote, "Yes, the latter part of my tour has given ample proof that the Gospel is still the power of God unto salvation. God is not only raising up groups of people in the towns and villages of the Gold Coast, but he is raising up among them individuals possessing spiritual vision and gifts. To the spiritual observer, not only the gifts of the Spirit are noticed, but the qualifying signs of the five-fold offices are in evidence. And it is to this end that we labour, that the church in Africa might be well furnished and lacking in no spiritual gift."[1]

James had a powerful mix of humility and authority. He knew he was called by God to do what he did. He had planted the initial seed. He was the father and undisputed head of the Church, but he also knew that his vision could only be fulfilled through others. He believed not only that God could use them, but that, unless he constantly gave them authority and encouraged them to take up responsibility, any gains made through his own work would be short-lived.

In the early days, leaders were hard to find and only a handful of pastors worked with James. Men were called to the pastorate by prophecy. In the late 1940s they were all champing at the bit, very zealous in wanting to fulfil what God was saying, but it was still a real struggle to go into the ministry. They were half afraid to go to prayer meetings in case a prophecy should call them to be pastors. If it did come, they often fought against it, because the life of a pastor was one of suffering and deprivation. "It was a very low standard of living and you would be carrying your bag up and down." James taught that a true leader should be willing to die for his flock and that the secret of success in ministry was in denying yourself and taking up the Cross. It even took such a man as M. K. Yeboah, the present chairman of the Church of Pentecost, three years before he accepted his call.

It was not only a matter of finding men willing to go, they had to be men of the right calibre, or sending them would be a waste of time. As James put it – "You could plant chaff or wheat, but only wheat would grow." When a pastor once complained that he was always being sent to spiritually dry areas, James' stinging reply was, "A fruitful person can make

1 Quoted in "The History of the Church of Pentecost" *op cit,* p 11.

good anywhere, but this man's dryness is revealed wherever he goes."

One of James's trusted men was Cofie Quaye who, back in Winneba, was the first African James had felt at one with in the Spirit. James had put something of himself into this man and soon Quaye became a deacon, then an elder. Quaye would tease himself, saying he was a young man just graduated from school, but by 1943 he was a full-time minister, opening up assemblies in many important towns. In 1948 he was ordained the very first prophet of the Church and by 1956, apostle. He was in the ministry 41 years and at one time, a third of the area of Ghana was his responsibility in the Church.

Pastor Paintsil was a brilliant, widely-read man who entered the ministry in 1948. He was a great asset to the Church and became its general secretary until his sudden death in 1981. However, most of the early leaders were not men of status and learning. For example, Pastor Asomaning had no education, but he was filled with the Spirit. If James asked him to interpret, Asomaning would spend the day in the bush, praying, "Father, you know I don't understand this man's language. Fill me with the Holy Ghost and let the Holy Ghost talk to the people." Eunice Addison said it was wonderful to see them together, preaching in the open air as Asomaning, through the Holy Spirit, interpreted James' words into his own language.

Other pioneer pastors – Hayford, Ankamah, Dufour, Gyimah, Bimpon, Boateng – were men of vision and dedication, but otherwise very ordinary Africans. James quoted, "Brothers, think of what you were when you were called. Not many of you were wise by human standards; not many were influential; not many were of noble birth. But God chose the foolish things of the world to shame the wise; God chose the weak things of the world to shame the strong. He chose the lowly things of this world and the despised things – and the things that are not – to nullify the things that are, so that no-one may boast before him." (1 Corinthians 1:26-29 NIV.) These ordinary men were willing to make the sacrifice to carry the Gospel – that extraordinary 'seed that splits rocks.'

Writing in 1949, James said, "Yes, the men have been found, and a willingness in their hearts to go at the command of their Lord. We have at present 16 men whom we have called from various departments of business life to devote themselves to the full-time ministry. Those who are placed in the coastal towns and these placed in the main centres of the interior, while they prove the presence of God with them, also realise the need for improvement in themselves to meet the needs of the educated."

Pastor Safo was still a boy when he decided to follow James as a disciple in the truest sense of the word. Eventually he became the next chairman of the Church. On committees, Pastor Safo behaved just like James. He would sit quietly, then come out with a couple of sentences of wisdom. The rest would then spend hours considering how to apply his words.

James taught that every true leader should be a man of worship, saying, "The beauty of Moses' life was that his face shone and he knew it not." That was a good description not only of James, but of Pastor Safo and of many of the other leaders we met as well.

Pastor Safo was the first Ghanaian I interviewed. It was our second day in Africa. He was lying on his side in a hospital bed, dying of cancer. Norman Barnes talked to him first. I felt out of my depth as I waited my turn. I had never before spoken to anyone who was the spiritual leader of a quarter of a million people. How could I communicate with this man? But he smiled and treated each of us, with great simplicity, as trusted friends. He would think before he spoke, but when his answers came they had rare qualities of depth, wisdom and honesty. In less than an hour I had learnt a wealth of things about the man, about the Church, about God. When a nurse came into the room, Pastor Safo explained who we were. "This is Norman Barnes. He has been to Ghana six times and has developed a special relationship with us. He has just arrived in our country and is aware that I am in hospital, but, even so, he and these brothers and sisters have chosen to come and visit me!" It was not a false humility. He was just like James in that he meant it. He was totally unaware that it was we who felt privileged to meet such a great man of God.

James gave something of himself which still lives on in Ghana. He also imparted gifts, which is one of the hallmarks of an apostolic ministry. To quote Eunice Addison again, "The power really rests with this man in the spoken word. As the Word comes out it breaks up and bears fruit in diverse colours." (He would say) 'Here in the Word you can prophesy,' 'You can go and heal.' Having imparted such a gift to someone, often through the laying on of hands, its successful use was not automatic, and James would not be content until he saw it worked out in their life and experience.

Many of the Church's leaders worked with James for years. Several were powerful enough to have split off and started their own work, yet very few did, despite the fact most of Ghana's indigenous churches are characterised by splits. Some of the long standing leaders explained how James always taught it was sinful to go away and start their own work. He explained that the only reason a branch is cut off a tree is if it is rotten. An arm or leg is only amputated if it is so diseased that it endangers the rest of the body. However, this is a serious matter, because the rest of the body will not function properly without it.

James told his leaders, "I trust in you. I want you to be faithful to me. You do not say you are faithful to God or to Jesus if you are not faithful to your friends!" Most European missionaries kept their native leaders under close supervision and, like school-boys in short trousers, they were never really trusted with things of importance. Eventually these men grew up and rebelled. James, remembering the farmers of County Antrim, never caused his spiritual children to defect or mutiny: he respected them and pushed more and more of the decision-making onto them. As they increased, he decreased and the Church learnt to trust and follow their African leaders. Outsiders were surprised, and the Apostolics were incensed when they found how James referred decisions to the Africans. However, they say a true leader is known not by what he leads, but by what he leaves behind. James left a Church which has grown faster than ever since he retired.

Rapid Church growth is a delightful problem to have, but it is nonetheless a real problem. In 1986, the opening of 269 new assemblies meant finding and training leaders for all of them. Apostle Nartey said, "Our greatest need at present is for leaders who are God-fearing to share the responsibility – so we will build not just another church, but the Church of God." In a time of plenty and harvest, the leaders have to hear and obey God just as much as in the leaner years.

If there is no clear training of the leaders, the mushrooming assemblies might well veer off in any number of strange directions, as has happened in many other African churches. The Church of Pentecost operates in such a way that leaders are trained right from conversion. In a local assembly, new converts will be called upon to give their testimony in public and to talk to their friends about Jesus. Ordinary Church members have opportunities to pray or sing at local Witness or Women's Movement meetings and they may be asked to practise preaching to a small meeting. Afterwards the congregation offers comments and advice. If leadership potential is recognised in terms of both gift and character, those people rise to be elders or deaconesses. This is how new leaders begin to grow into their responsibilities. They are proved in small situations before they are trusted with larger ones. From the newest convert up, everyone takes their responsibilities seriously – whether it be speaking in public, evangelising, music or administration. They do not wait for things to be organised for them. Not everyone has a timepiece – so there is no defined start to a meeting. As people begin to gather, they start to sing and to pray, irrespective of whether any leaders are there. As the noise grows, others realise it is time for the meeting and join in.

There is some formal training. Retreats for prayer and teaching are held from time to time by the pastor for his local officers, and for pastors and overseers within a region by the apostle. The Church of Pentecost General Council always starts with a couple of days of teaching, prophecy and prayer. David Mills, an Elim missionary, started a Bible centre for the Church of Pentecost in 1972. The idea was that each pastor should come for three or four months in-service training. Lionel Currie, also from Elim, has since taken over, but even today, there has not been time for all the pastors to attend even once, though men joining the full-time ministry now always start with a course there.

Other churches in Ghana have grown fast, then reached a plateau, due to a shortage of leaders. James vision from the beginning was to train and equip leaders at every level. Because the Church of Pentecost has continued to give this priority, so far they have contained their growth and continue to expand.

## Structure

One of the younger apostles, Opoku Onyinah, gave four reasons why the Church of Pentecost is the fastest-growing evangelical Church in West Africa – prayer, evangelism, discipline and structure. We have already looked at the first three. What is it about the structure of the Church which promotes growth?

If a tree had no structure and order, it would not be recognisable as a tree – there would be nothing to prevent its growth becoming grotesque and one-sided. As the Church expanded, it needed a structure. Even so, the formal side of the Church comes as something of a shock. Everyone is known by their title, never by their first name. Pastors swelter in Western suits and clerical collars. Are these symptoms of an exaggerated respect for leadership: or have attitudes of increasing informality in many UK churches taken us too far the other way? In a situation where there is little else to divert the attention, people need to be valued. Titles and special dress are a way of showing respect and worth. Of course, taken too far, formality leads to an inflexible structure which can obviate the need for God and to a pyramidal structure which can lead to an unhealthy vying for position.

James seemed to dislike formality and to have little interest in bureaucracy – he was much more concerned about hearing and doing what God said than following a set of rules. He would chair Church meetings, but even there, his contribution was to do with prayer and wisdom and the way he dealt with people. He said, "Africa needs God-given, Spirit-appointed leaders, not a constitution and bye-laws." The structure must have emerged as it did because the Africans felt secure in its formality. After all, they were used to living in the colonial system, where everything from health-care to education involved red tape, roll-calls, learning by rote, and obedient respect for leaders. If the Church had lacked a formal structure during the crucial period when Ghana has been emerging from colonialism, chaos might have ensued. Structure may change, however, as many of the younger leaders in the Church now seem to be thinking afresh about its organisation.

Briefly, the Church of Pentecost is structured like this. At the top comes the General Council of the Church which consists of most full-time workers plus some elders. It was set up back in 1948 and meets once a year. The seven man Executive Council can meet more often, but its decisions have to be ratified by the General Council.

The head of the Church is known as the chairman and acts like an executive president. James held this office until he retired. Next comes the general secretary, then apostles and regional heads. Pastors or overseers are in charge of districts of anything from ten to thirty assemblies. A presiding elder holds a secular job but is also in charge of a local assembly. He holds local presbytery meetings with the other local elders, deacons and deaconesses. From the grass roots up, decisions are made in the Church through local, district and regional presbytery meetings.

The Witness, Women's and Children's Movements have local, district, regional and national leadership. There is also a structure for finance, where regional deacons report to the Finance Board.

## Ministries

James talked about the way he was trying to encourage the 'five fold offices' which would build up the Church. Apostle Nartey said, "We need all five ministries – apostle, prophet, evangelist, pastor, teacher – so that people know where they are going." The apostles we met were not such in name only; they had pioneered new areas with the Gospel and planted churches in a way far beyond anything I had ever seen before.

An apostle, according to the Church of Pentecost, is someone with a wide area of ministry. He has received a call from God to open up new areas for the Church, ordain men to office, impart spiritual gifts to others and see there is discipline in the work. Apostles existed before the Church was divided into regions but now those who head regions are held responsible for all Church matters within that region. One apostle may be in charge of 500 assemblies, 34 pastors, 3,000 church officers and 45,000 people.

In Ashanti Region, we sat for hours in the apostle's house as he received a constant stream of people. We did not understand the language but, whether the visitor was a little child, the presbytery from a local assembly come to sort out some problem, or another apostle come to greet him, we noticed everyone was treated with the same attention and courtesy. I understood something David Mills said referring to James – in some ways he ran his administration like a tribal chief. This was how it must have been in the court of King David in the Bible – there was the same mixture of family accessibility and formal dignity. Again, it was African – this model of apostleship fitted their culture.

Similar functions to apostles are fulfilled by regional heads, who are men who may have the potential to become apostles. Pastor Safo explained, "Just like a fruit, we have to leave it on the tree to mature. We do not want to create a leadership vacuum: neither do we want to create a problem for that man, by giving him too much before he is ready."

Anyone in the Church of Pentecost can prophesy, but certain men have been recognised as prophets to the whole Church. Quaye was the first, but there have been about six, all-told. Today only two remain, and one was made first regional head, then chairman of the Church. Prophet Yeboah said that from the 1940s to the 1960s, men were normally called into the ministry through directive prophecy, but today prophetic utterance moves alongside other spiritual gifts, often confirming someone's call to the ministry. In the old days it was those who had the ministry of prophet who often gave specific direction to the Church, while other leaders acted as watchdogs to judge their prophecies. James had found the British Apostolics sometimes manufactured prophecies to confirm things that certain of them had already decided, and he was quick to stop any abuse of directive prophecy in Ghana.

There have been full-time evangelists, but normally this work is done by Pastors sent to what are called 'Missionary' or 'Liability' Districts, in or outside Ghana. It takes a long time to become a pastor. Today, three months at the Church of Pentecost Bible Centre is followed by two years as probationary overseer and another three as overseer, doing the same job as a pastor. At the end of this period comes ordination. Pastors and overseers work hard for little pay. Their wives usually try to earn some extra money to make ends meet. Pastors seldom have transport and walk miles around their districts, visiting established assemblies and opening new ones. Recently, one young pastor started with seven assemblies in his district. He had opened another five. Now, he felt sad. The reason? Every community in his area had its assembly and there was no more room for geographical expansion!

Today, pastors can be in charge of so many assemblies that historically they would have been considered to be apostles. The Church is keeping pace with its growth – but only just. Pastors, overseers and apostles have always moved to different stations around the country with extraordinary rapidity – again because of the rapid church growth. One man with particular talents might be called upon to sort out trouble in an area, or a district is split in two because it has grown so big, and a reshuffle of personnel results.

Really, the lynchpins of the Church are the elders, because no one man could fulfil the pastoral needs of up to 30 scattered assemblies. Elders tend to stay in one place where they have, in effect, a full-time job in the Church without any visible means of support. Their dedication and sacrifice is certainly on a par with that of the pastors. Men will normally be elders before going into the full-time ministry and it is a very good testing and training ground.

One strength of the Church is its system of accountability. Anyone can be dismissed – and there have been cases where even apostles were demoted or sacked. David Mills was astounded: in the first Council meeting he attended, an apostle was quizzed about why he had transferred a pastor. The previous year, this pastor had been moved away from the apostle, to encourage him to use initiative – now he was being moved back because he needed closer supervision. It was decided that the pastor was not showing initiative wherever he was stationed and he was dismissed, on three months salary, for gross inefficiency. David wondered just how many ministers back in the UK would stand that test, but he came to realise that high standards ensured a quality of ministry which has sustained the Church in Ghana.

# Chapter 11
# The Latter Rain

James concentrated on training African leaders, but he did not only work with Africans – the Apostolics sent other missionaries to help him as the Church grew. The first came to relieve James during his first furlough in 1939 – and promptly had a nervous breakdown. "He was a lovely man," said James, "and he had many qualities I lacked – but one thing he did not have was endurance." The next came in 1943. He and his family shared the large Cape Coast house with James and Sophia, but he caused all sorts of trouble over the years. Others followed, but none seemed to be able to relate to the Africans as James could. For example, another Apostolic missionary, Stanley Hammond, did a good work establishing the Witness Movement of the Church, but one Ghanaian commented, "He was not as friendly as James. We liked pleasant people who would play with us and enjoy us. James knew how to get round people."

The most successful Apostolic missionary who worked with James was his brother, Adam. He was to be very significant in the development of the Church. Born nine years after James, young Adam had asthma and bronchitis so badly he had to fight for breath, and did not know what it was to spend a whole night in bed. Still, he grew up good-looking and popular with the girls. Adam preferred playing with a dance band to anything spiritual until, one day, he found himself dying of pneumonia. His life changed dramatically as he met God, recovered, and started preaching. By 1944 he was an Apostolic pastor. The next year, James, at home on furlough, asked Adam if he had ever felt called to the mission field. Twelve years previously, God had told Adam he would serve abroad and the first place would be Africa.

James asked the missionary committee if Adam could

return to the field with him, but they had other plans. However, a few days later, one Apostolic prophet, who knew nothing of all this, prophesied that Adam McKeown should be sent to the Gold Coast. It was still war time, so Adam was forced to leave his wife and children at home when he sailed with James. As if to compensate, the first night on the ship, Adam had the first uninterrupted sleep of his life. God had healed him from lung trouble and it never returned.

The brothers sailed into Takoradi on VJ day. Adam wrote, "The whole harbour was a scene of jubilant celebration. All the ships were fully lighted up, rockets and fireworks lighted the sky. It was a night of joy ending six years of war." They stayed on board that night and disembarked the following morning. After Ireland, it all seemed strange to Adam. "Instead of the soft meadows and green fields, there were stretches of endless red sand. Instead of the fresh salty crisp air, with rain in the face, there was the hot, sticky, humid tropical climate of what was known as 'the white man's grave'. In our missionary meetings when we sang 'Where Afric's sunny fountains roll down her golden sands' it had sounded so very romantic, but this was for real. That night brought new sounds to my ears as the insects beat out their incessant rhythm."[1]

Adam stayed six months with James and Sophia in Cape Coast and then moved to Sekondi to superintend the Western Region, going off on treks into the bush, just as James had done. He missed his family, especially at Christmas time. The temperature was one hundred degrees, and he sat thinking of all the things that made Christmas at home so special, while the crooning voice of Bing Crosby on Sekondi radio sang 'I'm dreaming of a white Christmas'. Adam wrote, "You can guess how I felt. It is in moments like these that one requires more than the spirit of the martyr or of the heroic. It requires the deep inward assurance that

1 A Man Called Adam, *op cit.*

where you are, what you are doing, is in union with the heart and will of our heavenly Father."

By the next summer, Adam's family had joined him and they all settled in Accra from where Adam superintended the whole of Eastern Region. J. A. C. Anaman and A. S. Mallet were the pastors in charge of Accra at that time and the large church was packed to capacity. Adam decided to ease the congestion. He transformed the garage attached to his bungalow in Adabraka, making it into a small chapel. Within two weeks, so many neighbours had been converted in that part of Accra, their meetings overflowed to a nearby school.

A. S. Mallet's younger brother was a clerk in Accra post office. He was upset to have to leave the Church when work transferred him over fifty miles north to one of Eastern Region's main towns, Koforidua. He started preaching there, Adam went to lend a hand one weekend and decided to hold the district convention in the town. Adam wrote, "We notified all outlying stations in that part of the Province. They came by train, they came crowded into lorries, singing, clapping hands, playing tambourines, a sight Koforidua had never witnessed before. Many others walked for miles to make sure they would not miss the great event. Koforidua was never the same again.... On the final night of the convention I was greatly impressed by the people who came out – men and women, well-dressed, educated, many of them holding responsible positions in government and in the business world. In all, over 100 surrendered to the claims of the Gospel that night."[2]

News spread around the area and Adam was in demand, spending a large proportion of his time away from Accra. Within a few months, Koforidua Assembly numbered 500 and Adam was compelled to send them his right hand man – J. A. C. Anaman.

2 *Ibid*

Before Adam moved to Accra in 1946, a murder had been committed in the royal family of the native state of Akim Abuakwa. The ruler, based in Kibi, was one of the most powerful tribal chiefs in the country. Six men were sentenced to death, though all maintained their innocence. They were being held in Accra's Ussher Fort prison, whose superintendent was an African Christian called Mr Moses. This man often came to the Apostolic meetings and requested that James, who was on a visit to Accra, should go to the prison with Adam and Pastor Anaman. The missionaries met the six condemned men and were able to pray for them. Adam and Pastor Anaman continued to visit regularly and soon all six prisoners became Christians. Each time their execution was arranged, the church would pray and it would be put off for some reason.

In the end one of the older men died naturally. Three were executed. Two, however, had a dramatic last minute reprieve. Opoku Ahwenie and Amoaka Atta still had life sentences to serve and lost some of the privileges of access they had enjoyed as condemned men. The Keeper of the Prisons said that, if Adam could get converts in the prison, he would be allowed to continue as before, so the two "lifers" went to work, preaching the Gospel. Soon Adam was invited to preach to 20 new believers and found the 200 seat prison chapel filled. Later the men were so determined to hold a baptismal service, they formed a human chain, passing buckets of water to fill a large concrete trough. The other prisoners wanted to see this unusual event and the baptisms had a great impact on all concerned. Adam wrote, "From within those grim walls many went forth later, their lives transformed by the power of God, and became preachers of the Gospel to their fellow countrymen."

Amoaka Atta was then transferred to another Accra prison where the Warder was not so sympathetic, but Atta began to preach and Adam was invited to speak to the new converts. They were not allocated a room in which to do this, so they sang and preached in the open compound, a great opportunity to reach a captive audience! Soon a baptismal service was held in this prison also. By this time, Adam was holding two meetings a week in both prisons – but even more was to come from this unlikely source.

The Church held a memorial service for those who had been executed, which attracted many important people, including Dr. Danquah, who had been the lawyer for the condemned men. (Dr. Danquah was later the main contender against Nkrumah to become the first Prime Minister of independent Ghana.) Dr. Danquah was impressed and moved by the service. He was later imprisoned for his political beliefs, but became a Christian. Later he was found dead in his cell, in mysterious circumstances. The other sequel was that the two prisoners were later released and Opoku Ahwenie went on to become a pastor in the Church of Pentecost.

Adam did a good work during the two and a half years he was in the Gold Coast. Unlike some missionaries, he made many African friends but he was a very different man from James. Full of fun and jokes, an extrovert and a lively, fluent speaker – someone once commented that he would choose Adam to lead a meeting, but if he wanted a man to build a work, he would rather have James.

In 1948, Adam went on furlough. The Apostolics decided they did not want him to return to Africa, because they needed him in Canada. There, an Apostolic pastor called Fred Poole met Adam off the boat. Later, Poole introduced him to Dr. Thomas Wyatt, and this meeting was to have a great effect on the Apostolic Church in Ghana.

Dr. Wyatt, from Portland, Oregon, was a revivalist preacher who, in 1942, pioneered the first ever Christian healing programme broadcast on the radio. He was also involved in a movement called 'Latter Rain', which had started in Canada and was one of the precursors of the charismatic movement. Latter Rain brought an outpouring of the Holy Spirit and a restoration of the five-fold offices of apostle, prophet, pastor, evangelist and teacher. This was new to American Pentecostal circles, other than the Apostolics. On the other hand, the Apostolics had always kept themselves to themselves, while Latter Rain emphasised the unity of the body of Christ. There was also a strong emphasis against the sort of rigid, centralized organisation which had a stranglehold on American Pentecostalism at the time.

H. Cousen, the Apostolic missionary chairman back in Bradford, had a son called Cecil. As a young Apostolic pastor, Cecil was sent to Canada for two years. He heard Dr. Wyatt preach on faith there and it transformed his entire life and ministry. Cecil visited the main centre of Latter Rain in Detroit, and as soon as he walked through the door, thought, "This is what it used to be like when I was a boy in the Apostolic Church." It was the nearest thing to true revival he had seen.

Cecil was so impressed he suggested the Canadian Apostolics open their annual convention to the Latter Rain people and invite Dr. Wyatt to preach. Instead of 200 people they had 2,000. Instead of struggling to meet expenses, they had plenty of money left over and decided to send a team, headed by Dr. Wyatt, to Ghana and Nigeria. The rest of the team was made up of Adam McKeown, Fred Poole and Stanley Hammond (who was already an Apostolic missionary in Ghana.)

In the meantime, Cecil and the other Apostolic pastors in Canada were realising that some of their attitudes had been wrong. They had felt Apostolics were superior to other denominations. Now they had seen the Holy Spirit work in a new way, they no longer felt happy with all the Apostolic's rules and regulations or with the tight central control exercised from Bradford.

Cecil, Fred Poole and another man called George Evans returned to England and brought 'Latter Rain' to meetings up and down the country. This worried the Apostolic hierarchy so that, when they heard about Wyatt's proposed team visit to Africa, they were reluctant to allow it. James also was not keen on Wyatt's coming, forseeing it would cause trouble back home. However, his African Church Council very much wanted the team to come.

Politically, the Gold Coast was at boiling point. Nkrumah was calling for 'self government now'. Church members were affected by all the talk of imperialism and of how they were being downtrodden by Europeans. They were incensed that people in Bradford were trying to block this visit. Why should they be dictated to in this way? In the end, the team came at the invitation of the Church Council and, for just a few weeks in 1953, held meetings in Accra, Kumasi and Cape Coast. The Church was never to be the same again.

In Accra, a large canopy was erected to accommodate several thousand people, but it became evident it would not begin to hold the large crowds which gathered. Pastor A. S. Mallet, an electrician, installed an additional PA system which carried the sound to those on the outside. Dr. Wyatt preached and a well-known Methodist businessman, who had been partially paralysed by a stroke, applying the words to himself, rushed up to the platform and nearly knocked Fred Poole over with an arm which had been lifeless before. A crippled beggar, a familiar figure in the city, was so overcome by what he saw, he too rushed onto the platform and the two of them were dancing and leaping and praising God.

So it began and so it went on day after day, as thousands gathered to hear the Word of God and see His power demonstrated. The lame walked, the blind saw, the deaf heard and the dumb sang the praises of God. The meetings needed no advertising and there was great joy, all around the city and further afield, as hundreds were saved.

In Kumasi thousands of people attended each night. After every meeting they would pray for the sick with the laying on of hands, but by far the most miracles happened as the Word was preached. Even sick people from a nearby leper colony were made whole. In Cape Coast it was the same, the miracles, the freedom in worship, the sense of the presence of God was bringing a new revival to this already lively Church and new Christians were being added daily.

# Chapter 12
# Overcomers

When I first approached James about writing this book, he was not at all keen on the idea. "There were splits," he said, "I hate splits – I do not want all those things from the past dragged up again." A year later, the Church of Pentecost in Ghana wrote their own brief Church history which focuses in far more detail than I shall do on these events. Realising it was all out in the open anyway, James consented to talk, but avoided mentioning the names of people who had caused trouble or betrayed him.

In Ghana, there were no such scruples – for once the Ghanaians disagreed with James. "God does not hide attacks. The Bible does not tell us only about nice people – we read of things that go wrong in order that we can learn from them. It would not be right to let people assume the Church experienced no internal difficulties. The point is that whatever disaster seemed to befall us, as we remained true to what God had said, a stronger Church emerged the other side."

Right from the beginning in Asamankese, there were difficulties to be overcome, but some words which James wrote around 1945 turned out to be prophetic, "Eight years ago, how comforting were the words, 'Can these bones live?' The call was for faith in the Word. When the tender life did appear, 'Can it survive?' was the question. God is good, the tree has grown; from the branches there hangs fruit. But there are still birds in the air and they want a place to nest. There are still snakes in the grass and they want the little birds, so they have to climb the tree. There are many insects – they want the fruit. There are diseases carried by the insects who feed on the life of the fruit. 'Can God preserve and keep that which has been planted from all these evils?' "

Eight years on from 1945, James worried that Dr. Wyatt's visit to the Gold Coast would lead to conflict with the Apostolics back home and he turned out to be right. The root of the problem was not with Dr. Wyatt, nor was it with the Gold Coast Church. The Apostolics had very strict central control. The sect has been called "The most authoritarian and hierarchical structure in British Pentecostalism."[1] It was rare for an outsider to be allowed to speak to Apostolic meetings, rules and regulations covered every eventuality. The UK Apostolics seemed to have become bound by their own constitution. Into this situation, Cecil Cousen and his friends tried to bring the freedom of Latter Rain.

Every four years, the Apostolics held a Council which was the final authority of the church. All their pastors and missionaries were required to return from their stations to attend. In May 1953, the Quadrennial Council spent several days discussing the Latter Rain, first all that had happened in the UK, then in Canada and finally in the Gold Coast. In an effort to make sure no-one from outside the Apostolics ever again visited their work without the approval of home base, amendments were made to the constitution. One of these created separate apostles for whites and blacks, so that a black apostle could not exercise authority over a white person.

The 54 Council members present were asked to re-affirm this revised constitution. One by one they did so. James McKeown and Cecil Cousen were the only men to refuse. James stood and quietly said that he felt the amendments were unscriptural, so he could not, out of a pure conscience, subscribe to them. James and Cecil were told to hand in their ordination certificates and leave. No Apostolic platform in the world would be open to them in future. Stunned and disorientated, they walked to Cecil's house. It was perhaps

1 Andrew Walker, *Restoring the Kingdom* (Hodder and Stoughton: London, 1985), p 241.

worse for Cecil, who had known no church but the Apostolics. James had never been happy with their more extreme elements. Though James had little time for denominationalism, he said that, on reflection, he had always felt more in tune with the Elim Band of his youth.

Back in the Gold Coast, the Africans were dismayed when news of James' dismissal filtered through. They had found nothing but great good in Latter Rain and could not see how it conflicted with either Scripture or Apostolic doctrine. They wanted James to return as their superintendent, but realised this could not happen if they remained in the Apostolics. They took a unanimous decision to sever relations with Apostolic missionary headquarters at Bradford and ask James back on their own responsibility. So now there was an independent African Church led by James, which was known as 'The Gold Coast Apostolic Church'. However, the British Apostolics, or 'Bradfords' as they became known in Africa, did not want to give up their work in the Gold Coast so easily. They sent in more missionaries to head the 'Apostolic Church, Gold Coast', which was controlled from the UK. The similarity in names was to cause much confusion.

A few people left James to join the 'Bradfords', who then started litigation to claim church money and buildings for themselves. Because James had always insisted on internal African finance, these things had never belonged to the UK Apostolics in the first place, yet ironically, though it kept most of the people, James's Church was to lose most of the buildings and money. Large churches which now belonged to the Bradfords were standing almost empty, while crowds of James' followers met wherever they could. Still, James would not be diverted from his primary aim – evangelism. He refused to put much effort into property, saying God would help the people with that.

In the wake of the Latter Rain visit, some Americans connected with Dr. Wyatt set up a Bible school in the Gold

Coast, teaching that money should be decentralised and evangelists be responsible for baptising their own converts. In Africa, this freedom tended to bring chaos. The Church lost a few pastors and 31 out of its 512 assemblies over the issue.

The Latter Rain had introduced the Holy Spirit to vast numbers of people in the Gold Coast. They were added to the Church, including some leaders from other churches. Later, however, some of the pastors who had joined because they were attracted by the work of the Holy Spirit split off to form works of their own. These included churches like the Divine Healers, or the Apostolic Reformed, which still have a vigorous existence in Ghana today.

Despite all the difficulties, as James's Church obeyed God and pressed on with evangelism, they proved God was faithful. From 1956 onwards James's 'Gold Coast Apostolic Church' was easily the leading Pentecostal church in the country.

A WEC missionary I talked to had worked in Ghana since the early 1970s. Looking at the situation from outside the Church of Pentecost, he commented what an amazing influence James had on Ghana. "People do not often realise that half the churches in Ghana owe a lot to James McKeown and have their roots in his Church. Because of the splits, people sometimes dismiss all the good he did, assuming he caused trouble by being awkward and refusing to fit in with others. In reality, he was a man who knew where he was going and he would not be diverted. He moved according to Scripture, without any preconceived ideas and never looked over his shoulder to see what others thought of what he was doing. Whatever the crisis, he refused to compromise with the truth. The splits occurred only because he was trying to keep the Church pure and on course."

To be fair, very few missionaries of James's stature have planted churches on a grand scale while under the control of a home-based church or missionary society. Such men need the freedom to hear the Spirit of God on the spot.

James was among the first to teach about the Baptism of the Holy Spirit in the Gold Coast. Then, his Church was scorned and despised for its Spirit-filled worship. Now, it is commonplace in Ghana, right across the spectrum from Roman Catholics to University Christian Unions.

James simply did what God had told him to, with no compromise. Being a radical, ahead of his time, meant that some religious people fought against him. He was strict and uncompromising about moral issues, which made him unpopular also with those who welcomed the good news about salvation but were not so keen to change their lives.

By 1960, worse trouble brewed. In the wake of Ghana's independence in 1957, the second-in-command of the Church, J. A. C. Anaman, decided it should have an African chairman. When James was out of the country, Pastor Anaman wrote to him, saying President Nkrumah had decreed churches must be led by Africans. James accepted this and Anaman became chairman, but when James returned to Ghana, he found out Nkrumah had ordered no such thing. It was all a plot by Anaman and a few others to oust their chairman. James remembered that when he first ordained elders back in 1939, he had prophesied that Anaman would betray him. The Church was badly shaken, but most people took James's side and James drew strength from the many who stood by him through all these troubles. Anaman eventually left to join the Bradfords, but all sorts of false rumours continued to spread about James. He was vilified on the radio and in the press, brought before the civil courts and threatened with expulsion from the country. No true complaint could be made against him and those who knew him defended him, even at Governmental level. It became a matter of national importance and President Nkrumah himself became involved in 1962, resolving all the disputes about property and pronouncing James free to stay in the country and to head the Church. President Nkrumah also decreed that the confusion over names should end. From August, 1962, 'The Gold Coast Apostolic Church' became known as 'The Church of Pentecost.'

James was an emotional man. He was wounded by trusted friends who betrayed him and remained upset by the splits which tarnished the image of the Church. On the other hand, though, he once said, "The one who realises the depths of the call of God is burdened and at times feels lonely, but is never filled with worries and complaints and grievances." James knew he had been called by God and, even through the worst times, never lost sight of the fact that God is building His Church and the gates of Hell cannot prevail against it. In the final analysis, James was not a man who let his emotions rule him. His attitude was – if the Church cannot be clean before God without some splitting away, then so be it!

There were difficult times and they have left their mark on the Church, but, as Apostle A. T. Nartey pointed out, "God knows what He is doing. We thought the Church was going to fall apart, but instead it became stronger. When Joseph's brothers sold him into slavery, it seemed like a disaster, but God was preparing him for a purpose. We lost buildings, money and people, but the Lord gave us back a hundred-fold and our new buildings are all full!"

The Church of Pentecost has learnt what it is to stand firm and prove God's words true. The joy the Ghanaian Christians have, even in difficulties, is something many of us could learn from. The Church is a strong Church partly because it has overcome all the many obstacles and divisions in its history. But more than that, living in a Third World country, surviving famine and disease, learning to trust God literally for their daily bread, they have found a joy which survives hardship. Back in England, Norman Barnes treasures an especially beautiful piece of African cloth. Its owner had told Norman about how his farm had been destroyed by fire during the drought, "But I'm still praising God," he said, and meant it. Norman commented how well the man looked in his cloth and the next day it was presented to him – its value equivalent to the man's earnings for much of the year. We can read stories about church growth with great excitement, but there is always a price to pay. Africa's remarkable overcomers continue to pay it joyfully.

# Chapter 13

# The Tree Becomes a Forest

God works in His own way. He sent Jesus as a baby, not as some powerful cosmic force to save the world. He designed nature so that things are rarely born with a big bang. Beginnings seem insignificant – even a forest starts with a few tiny seeds. But who could have guessed from the seeds that an Irishman planted in the lives of ordinary people, that a Church would grow faster than a forest, in West Africa?

Those first few believers whose lives were transformed through James's ministry were mainly women, meeting in small groups near Cape Coast or in remote parts of the Western Region of the Gold Coast. Africans think nothing of travelling and it is not easy to trace the geographical spread as these women gossiped the Gospel around the market places of the towns they happened to visit. Early-on came a self-propagation to the large western port of Takoradi-Sekondi. By 1945, Kumasi (capital of Ashanti and the second most important town in the Gold Coast) had an assembly which was neither started nor run by James, but which came within his control. From there, the Africans reached out and, in 1946, Cofie Quaye was moved to be in charge of the Church in Ashanti. The early pastors were few and at this stage, were transferred around the country at an alarming rate, as new areas opened up and needed supervision.

D. Y. A. Owusu, with a handful of others, preached the Gospel in Brong Ahafo in the late 50s and early 60s. Many of the two million people in this large and comparatively remote region to the north and west of Ashanti had never heard about Jesus before. In one year, 1972, the 4,332 Church of Pentecost members in the region made 1,012 converts – a phenomenal growth rate! By 1986, there were over 23,500 members in 342 assemblies in Brong Ahafo and the Church's region had to be split in two for administrative purposes.

Some areas proved more difficult. A century earlier, the Akwapim hills, an hour's car ride from Accra, had been the first area successfully evangelised by Presbyterian missionaries, but the region was also controlled by a very strong fetish power. No other church could make any headway there. Then one of James's young men called F. D. Walker (Ghanaian despite the name) started to evangelise and soon there were many thriving new assemblies.

Other difficult areas were Volta Region in the east, where there was a concentration of occult activity and the Northern and Upper Regions of the country, where Islam predominates. The Church in Volta Region is growing now, but the north remains a difficult area. Nothing happened there until 1953. Then Pastor Apau Asante was called, by name, in a prophecy, to take "his wife, his three children, belongings, accordion and voice" and settle in a central northern town called Tamale. Though it is much hotter in the north, Apau Asante obeyed and found ten Christians there, all migrants from the south. Apau Asante stood on the street corners, trying to attract attention with his accordion and his wife played the cymbal, but evangelism was hard. The people spoke a different language and most in the town were Muslims. He found that Islam had not reached all the surrounding villages, and here the Gospel gained a foothold. By 1958, nine northern towns had assemblies and 5,000 attended the region's convention – a remarkable achievement.

Today, 20% of Ghana's population claim to be Muslims. There is a battle on in Ghana, as Islam spreads southwards and its converts resist Christianity. Only five of the current Church of Pentecost pastors are northerners, and the different languages and traditions of the north make it difficult for a pastor originating from the south to communicate effectively there.

Ghana now has Church of Pentecost assemblies in all its major towns and most villages. Once the seeds had been planted in people's lives, the ground was fertile. Like the seeds sown in good ground in Jesus's parable, they yielded sixty-or a hundred-fold. We had to walk over an open sewer outside one assembly in Kumasi. The building was packed to capacity and there were more seats under an awning outside. The people here were nearest the sewer; they could not actually see what was going on in the service, yet the seats were full. We thought this was remarkable enough, until we were told this assembly had spawned others. When, as now, the building physically overflowed with people, some of them would be formed into a new assembly, meeting elsewhere in Kumasi. This has happened no less than sixty times in forty years! As we drove through that large city, we must have passed a Church of Pentecost building every half mile or so.

Each Church of Pentecost region has soul-winning targets for the year. These are often based on the number of converts made the previous year, yet there seems to be no trouble reaching them. For example, the target for 1975 in Greater Accra was 500. By the end of the year they had 1540 new converts – exceeding their goal three times! These converts were included in the total regional membership of just 9,395.

Today, evangelism is on a massive scale. Every Church member is involved and over 4,000 evangelistic rallies were held in 1985. Between 1970 and 1980, Church of Pentecost membership more than doubled and the number of assemblies increased by almost 100%. Today they open an average of five new assemblies a week, all over Ghana. For example, in Ashanti Region, by January 1987, there were 450 assemblies. The pastors prayed and set a target of 500 by the end of the year. More prayer and a survey of the area gave them various places to target and groups of around eight people were sent to preach the Gospel. More became involved, then the nearest Church of Pentecost assembly held a rally in the place. A different pastor every week, for six to eight weeks, stayed among the new converts, helping and teaching them. At the end of this time, local elders were appointed and the new assembly established, under the oversight of a full-time district pastor. Ashanti region reached their target of a ten percent growth rate in just nine months. Three months ahead of schedule, the Church had fifty new assemblies in that one region.

There is still plenty of room for growth in Ghana, with only ten percent of the population being committed Christians, but, in 50 years, those seeds James planted have undeniably changed the face of Christianity in the country.

## Going into other nations

Boundaries of nations in West Africa are in many ways artificial, drawn on the map by the colonial powers when they divided the area among themselves. The people have always been used to migrating over long distances and still do so. In this way seeds are carried by Church of Pentecost members into neighbouring countries. Fishermen, who migrate along the coast, share their faith and, before long, have a small group of new believers on their hands. They then ask for visits or permanent pastoral help from home base.

From the 1950s on, James's Church had a sizeable missionary outreach to other countries, so they started having monthly missionary prayer meetings and offerings. The missionaries are far too busy to go around the home assemblies, drumming up support as missionaries do in the UK. People in Ghana might well never have heard of Pastor So-and-So in Liberia, yet they trusted the leaders and gave faithfully, easily meeting all the needs.

James himself went with Pastor Paintsil to Nigeria, Cameroun, Liberia, Côte d'Ivoire, Togo, Benin, and Upper Volta. They would preach, appoint local elders, investigate any problems and see if any further help was required. James was never conventional. The Apostolics had a large and well-established mission field in Nigeria and James was friendly with the missionary-in-charge, George Elton. This man had been on the ship when James first went out in 1937 and he asked James to visit and keep an eye on things while he was on furlough.

In this, one of his first expeditions outside the Gold Coast, James found himself in a Nigerian town called Ilesha. When the people gathered for a meeting, James noticed several toothless old women. Choosing the oldest and ugliest he could find, he lined them up at the front. He told them, "You look like you have lived a long time and the Devil has had a good crack at you! Remember Samson? He had no eyes, yet in his death, he killed all those Philistines. Now come on out and start to sing." It was usual for nice, well-dressed girls to form a choir. These old people were delighted that they had been asked and so were their children and grandchildren. "What a meeting we had! It was a real break-through in Nigeria," said James, "but remember, it was my own way. You don't think I learned that in Bible school!"

James found that an American missionary, who was supposed to be working for Elton, was continually speaking against his boss. Having written a letter to Elton, telling him what was going on, James showed it to the American. "What we say behind people's backs we must say to their face," James explained, "If I find this sort of thing, I will expose it." The missionary returned to America.

After the split with the Apostolics, James's Church had little to do with **Nigeria** until the late 1970s. Most Church of Pentecost members then were expatriate Ghanaians and in 1982, the Nigerian government issued an Aliens Compliance Order which sent all foreigners home. The Church of Pentecost was left with just 41 members in 3 assemblies in the country. The Church came close to being shut down but, by 1986, there were 10 assemblies, nearly all of whose 360 members were Nigerian.

**Togo,** immediately to the east of Ghana, was one of the earliest nations in which James's Church took root. By 1954, they had a Togolese pastor and some American missionaries came to help him there, supported by Dr. Wyatt. All was not well, however. The terrain and transportation posed problems, but worse, when James visited in 1957, he found the Togolese pastor mishandling money, and dismissed him. Also, the senior American was having fellowship with other American missionaries from the Assemblies of God in such a way that the Togolese Church members thought he was turning against them. By contrast, one of the things the Africans liked about James was that he associated almost exclusively with them. "If you've come to us, be with us," they would say, "and don't carry stories about us to other white people."

Because of leadership problems, James could see the Church in Togo was in a mess. Financially, it was a liability and there was mistrust among the leadership. Pastor Safo took over and in a short time a barren land became fruitful. "You have to get your man and then everything else will follow," said James. "Pastor Safo did not know the language, but I trusted him from the beginning."

People would travel a long way to meetings in Togo. Pastor Safo said, "In those days you knew you had arrived at a convention by the pile of bikes outside. People did not charter transport then. They would walk, or use a push-bike or 'motorette'. It was quite a sight, four people sitting on one bike – Father pedalling for many miles, the mother astride the cross-bar with a baby on her back and a little boy in the carrier – all of them happy and singing because they were on their way to the convention!"

By 1978, the Togo Church topped 4,000 members, but then the Togolese government had a row with the Ghanaian one and banned any church whose headquarters was in Ghana. The Church carried on meeting in secret. There was persecution and sometimes whole congregations were arrested. Still, by 1986, though the Church did not officially exist and the border with Ghana was often closed, there were 6,525 members in 147 assemblies all over the country.

**Benin** (formerly called Dahomey) lies next to Togo and the Church in the two countries began at about the same time, when small groups of Ghanaian fishermen moved there. By 1957, Pastor Anaman reported that some people travelled as many as 64 miles to attend services in Dahomey. Later the government closed the borders, and allowed only Beninians to hold office, which was a problem, as there had always been close administrative links with the Church in Togo. In addition, Church assets were frozen and their activities banned in some areas. Even at this time, their converts were numbered in hundreds. Today the situation is easier and 1986 figures show 3,392 members in 57 assemblies in Benin.

In **Côte d'Ivoire,** (the Ivory Coast) immediately to the west of Ghana, the Church also started through people migrating from the Gold Coast in the 1950s and in 1986 it had over 2000 members in 81 assemblies.

**Burkina Faso,** (formerly Upper Volta) lies to the north of Ghana and has similar problems to that region, in that many of its population are Muslims. Work there started in the late 1950's and for a while it was administered jointly with the Church in north Ghana. Progress has been slow and difficult and, by 1985, the Church had just 7 assemblies and 638 members.

Much more dynamic has been the progress made in **Liberia,** to the west of Côte d'Ivoire. Some Ghanaian fishermen settled there and requested help from headquarters. Growth was phenomenal. In one region of the country there were just 70 members, yet when Pastors Paintsil and Walker visited, 59 were baptised in water, and 33 in the Holy Spirit.

Pastor F. D. Walker, who had already evangelised the

Akwapim area of Ghana, was sent to be the first permanent pastor in Liberia. He was given just $400 and, when he asked James for a PA system, was told the apostles Peter and Paul never had one! Someone asked if he were not even going to take a camp bed but Pastor Walker was resigned, "I don't know where I shall stay, I might as well trust God for a bed too!" He had no hope of finding accommodation in the capital, Monrovia, but on arrival, found the fishermen had secured him a room there. The only problem was the monthly rent – at $410, more than the total of his resources! "I had to seek God," he said.

The fishermen wanted to go to the main Church of Pentecost convention, which, in 1975, was held in Cape Coast, Ghana. The men worked a poor fishing area and had no money for transport, so they asked Pastor Walker to pray. Suddenly they landed huge catches and were, in fact, so successful, that the market for that type of fish was soon saturated. Pastor Walker asked them to specify another kind. They prayed and soon their nets were full of these new fish. When they reached Cape Coast, the men were able to show photographs of the modern-day miracle bursting out of their nets.

The work grew and eventually they needed a church building. There seemed no way of getting one, so they fasted and prayed, then Pastor Walker went to see the Head of State who was a Christian. He was sympathetic and prayed with them, but could do nothing more, as the land was privately owned. Pastor Walker was convinced they would get a plot in a certain area, but the church members laughed and said this was impossible. Two weeks later, one came up for sale in just that place. Somehow, they gathered a few coins here and a few there, until they could pay the first instalment. The money continued to arrive in very small amounts until they had paid it all off and the church they built was their own. By 1985, there were 1,300 members in 18 assemblies and by the time we were in Ghana, the Liberian branch of the Church of Pentecost had started their own missionary outreach into the country on the other side of them – **Sierra Leone.**

Most recently, the Church has been registered in **The Gambia,** all the more remarkable because it is a predominently Muslim country.

Missionary work was simpler before Independence. The colonial powers were normally in favour of it and there was no trouble with foreign exchange because the Gold Coast used sterling. Because the Ghanaian currency has no value outside the country, the people there have to look to God, encourage migrants to spread the Gospel, and pray for stability in their own government so that the financial situation may improve. There have been many prophecies in recent years to the effect that God has set the Church of Pentecost as a light to evangelise Africa.

James always had a vision for Africa, but his travel was not limited to that continent. After the split with the Apostolics he had more to do with Dr Wyatt and two of his own brothers, who lived in North America. James went there on five or six preaching tours, from the early 60s through to the late 70s – travelling widely around the continent, from Oregon to Ontario. Typically, he set the cat among the pigeons by insisting on staying with black people whenever he could!

James was used to pick-up trucks and trams, but had limited experience of driving a car. In America, an Irishman got him through the test on the strength of being Irish, but James was not used to snow and he skidded on the way to a meeting, sending the car down a 12 foot embankment. Miraculously, no-one was hurt.

James went to Mrs Bealle's church in Detroit, where the Latter Rain movement had begun. He stood to preach on the text 'Spring up, O well' (Numbers 21:17 AV) but the missionary first got all the congregation singing. The Spirit so came upon the meeting that James never had the chance to preach. The church always remembered this and asked him back on future tours.

## Links with the wider church

James had an open door to North America, and his Church was spreading like a forest across West Africa, but no one church has sole access to God. The Church of Pentecost in Ghana had split from its roots, they wanted to feel a part of the world-wide church again.

David and Margaret Mills were English missionaries pioneering for Elim in Ghana. They were based in Koforidua, a town of about 30,000 people, which already had a total of sixteen different Pentecostal denominations. The Mills had 200 people and a lot of heartache to show for three years hard work and seriously questioned what they were doing in the country.

Just before the Mills's first leave in 1969, the whole of the Church of Pentecost gathered in Koforidua for its general convention. This came to David and Margaret's attention when the town's population was doubled over-night. They went to a meeting feeling disillusioned and sceptical but the sight of so many Ghanaians praising God, acted on them like a tonic. They were soon joining in the worship, which they found tremendously exciting. In Ghana, Margaret wore a towelling nappy around her neck, to mop up perspiration. She joined in the dancing and waved her nappy when the Ghanaians waved their hankies! Then James preached for 75 minutes. David (who had been invited to sit on the platform) scanned the congregation of 35,000 for signs of inattention – and found none.

Then James did something he seldom did before or since, he asked David, then a stranger to him, to preach the next night. "What an experience!" David remembered, "100 leaders sat on the platform behind me, urging me on, almost preaching the sermon for me. Immediately afterwards, 167 people came to know Jesus. Over 2,000 Church members came forward in response to God's speaking to them through the sermon. I didn't know what had hit me! I had found Ghanaians difficult to work with, but here something was obviously different. I wanted to know what was behind it – so I asked if I could come to their Council meeting and that was a revelation to me – the budget, the way discipline was accepted, the reports of the regional heads, everything."

At the end, James took those who were in the Executive Council off for a special meeting and suggested the rest spend the time listening to David and asking him questions. When James returned, he said to the Council, "Well, now you have heard David. He represents Elim. Last year you said you would like affiliation with a church overseas, so you would feel a part of something bigger. How about an affiliation with Elim?"

David was flabbergasted, but he was also impressed with James. There was something about him which was more than the physical presence of a powerful, upstanding man, more than force of personality. Though James spoke very quietly, David recognised tremendous power in his words – as well as good sense. Here was a man who spoke with authority!

Another difference was that James seemed to have a genuine care for people. After the meeting, scores of Africans milled round as they waited to greet James. Not only did James greet them all by name, he asked in great detail after their families. David realised this was quite extraordinary in such a large convention.

David soon found himself with James at Elim headquarters in Cheltenham, talking about a merger. James, however, pulled no punches and when someone from Elim asked, "Why can't we be one now?" James replied, "I'm speaking to intelligent gentlemen. Before there is a successful marriage, do you not think there should be a courtship?" They just laughed. James continued, "I've heard that Elim is so stiff. How do you think you could come together with a bad man like James McKeown and be a success?"

The two did become affiliated. David and Margaret became great friends of James and Sophia and had very fruitful ministries among the Ghanaians. David set up the Church of Pentecost's Bible centre for training pastors and ran it for many years. He also pastored a district near Kumasi which in his time grew from 62 members to over 6,000. Margaret set up the Children's Movement in the Church, travelling all over Ghana and West Africa. This started in 1972 and by 1986 involved 71,000 children in Ghana alone.

Other links with Elim include more missionaries – the Curries, for example, are a British couple who replaced the Mills in 1984. There are regular visits – two of the UK Elim Executive were touring the various Church of Pentecost conventions when we were in Ghana. The traffic is not all one way – quite a few of the Ghanaian leaders have ministered in the UK. Of course, the Church of Pentecost dwarfs Elim in terms of sheer numbers. In 1985, Elim's general convention in the UK drew 4,000 as against the Church of Pentecost's 125,000. The Church of Pentecost is a real giant and dwarfs any UK denomination in terms of growth. Historically, British Christians have had great input to churches abroad, but the situation is changing. Though there may be contributions in terms of skills that Christians in the UK have to offer, we have so very much to learn from the Africans. Some may well come as missionaries to this country.

Earlier, the Ladlows came out as Elim missionaries and helped set up the radio ministry of the Church and the radio programmes provoked great interest in Ghana. In '1980 alone, the radio pastor's office received 8,000 letters. At least one assembly was started as a direct result of radio evangelism. When we were in Ghana, however, all sponsored religious programmes were off the air by order of the government.

As the Church has grown, other forms of communication have become more sophisticated. Elim donated a press in 1975 which prints the Church's magazine, *Pentecost Fire* as well as thousands of tracts in various languages.

In 1979, Norman Barnes went to Ghana as a result of a contact he had made in another church there. Just before leaving England, he happened to meet the Ladlows, who gave him the Mills's address in Kumasi. Things did not go well for Norman. For two weeks he consumed untreated Ghanaian food and water. His bed was so hard, he was covered in bruises. At this time Norman went to tea with the Mills's who opened a tin of meat-balls from their precious stock. Meat was expensive, so one meat-ball each was a real treat for them. David and Norman immediately took to each other, and, worried about Norman's living conditions, David invited him to stay. Norman was amazed at what he saw in the Church of Pentecost. He was asked to speak in the 5,000 capacity McKeown Temple in Kumasi and when he arrived, realised that it fulfilled a vision he had when he was 16. He was speaking to thousands of people and the hymns, the order of service, the building itself, all matched his vision exactly.[1]

When Norman returned to England, he began sending supplies to the Mills and 'Links International' was born. This has since bought vehicles, a printing machine, workshop, literature, tapes etc for the Church of Pentecost. These are all things for which hard currency is needed. People with medical or engineering skills have been sent on short-term service – and speakers too. Links International has gone on to help churches in other Third World countries in similar ways. Norman has visited Ghana almost every year since 1979, often with his wife, Grace, and others. Everyone who

1 This story is told more fully in the book, *God gave me a Dream,* by Norman Barnes with Rod Boreham, (New Wine Press, 1988.)

has been would say that they received from these African Christians far more than they could give.

Another fairly recent link the Church of Pentecost has made with the wider church, is through being an active member of the Ghana Pentecostal Council, which is made up of Ghana's larger Pentecostal denominations. It is similar to the Evangelical Alliance in that such a sizeable body can have quite an influence on the nation, especially should governmental decisions or practice go against Christ's teachings in any way.

Now that the Church of Pentecost is so big, and involved in so much, the administration is formidable, but is handled efficiently by the large staff at Head Office in Accra and by the regional offices. The structure has to support the 'trees' of the church 'forest' without restricting growth – always a difficult area in any church and critical at this time in the Church of Pentecost's history.

James always said that evangelism came first and that, once the Church was strong, it would be in a position to help the country in other ways. Now the Church has a strong spiritual, administrative and financial base, it runs several schools and farms and two mobile clinics. Again, Elim and Links have sent out hard currency and personnel to help establish these. The Church of Pentecost itself gives to many charities within Ghana, such as children's homes, mental hospitals and leprosy missions. At one time the majority of the Church's income went on pastor's salaries: now a large percentage is given away to social relief projects right outside its own jurisdiction.

PENTSOS (or Church of Pentecost Social Services) is the organisation which co-ordinates giving towards the social and economic growth of the country. PENSA (or Pentecost Students and Associates) aims to meet the needs of the more highly educated Ghanaians. These are two of the newer branches of the Church which show its growth is not just in terms of numbers or geography, but reaches across every strata of society. Over 2% of Ghana's population belong to the Church of Pentecost. As individuals, Church members are in all sorts of jobs and, by the small choices they make every day, are pushing standards a little bit more towards those of God's Kingdom.

The Church of Pentecost grows with the speed and vigour of a tropical forest, covering length, depth, breadth and height. Branches and roots shoot off in all directions, changing the face of the land, providing shelter and protection for the weak and helpless, food and a whole environment to those who choose to commit themselves to Jesus. When James was first in the Gold Coast, he loved the huge forest trees which shaded the paths he walked and the places where he prayed. After Independence, he saw that forest dwindle. Greedy men cut down the timber giants but did not replant and the country no longer looks the same. The Church is conscious of the need to pray it is never destroyed by men in a similar way, but, obeying only Jesus, that it is able to stand strong against all attacks and maintain the momentum of its remarkable growth.

# Chapter 14
# "Yet Greater Things..."

The last chapter saw the Church right up to date, but what happened to James and Sophia? They retired to obscurity in Northern Ireland.

Sophia, being six years older than James, was the first to move. Though she had a house-girl in Ghana, Sophia insisted on doing most domestic work herself. Whenever anyone called, she would run to the kitchen and prepare food for them. Obstinately, she hand-washed and pressed all James's shirts, because she liked to believe he was fussy. James worried about his wife as she grew older. He felt she was wearing herself out and becoming distressed. She would not stop being busy, and it took so much out of her. In 1974, James decreed that life in Ghana was too much for his wife and that she must return to Northern Ireland. Sophia did not want to leave. She cried, but out of submission to her husband, she did as he said. From a gift given by the Ghanaians, together with another sum a British man had held in trust for them, the McKeowns were able to buy a modern, two-bedroomed bungalow. So it was that they moved to a pleasant cul-de-sac on the outskirts of Ballymena, the county town of Antrim.

From 1974 until 1982, James's heart was divided. He would spend much of the year with Sophia, returning to Ghana only for three or four months around the time of the Council. There, he would grow increasingly restive, wondering how Sophia was coping without him: but when he was in Ireland, he worried about the Church he had left behind. James regretted the long absences from his wife and wondered if he made the right decision in sending her home. Sophia deteriorated rapidly as soon as she left Ghana. She returned once, in 1977, and laid the foundation stone of the huge

'Sophia McKeown Temple' in Labadi, Accra. By then the tropical heat, which was never a problem all the time she lived in Ghana, had become intolerable to her.

James said his love for his wife increased as the years went by and that he found something even more beautiful in her as she grew older. Realising that he had been "a better missionary than he was a husband", James found new ways of expressing his love for Sophia. Long ago, before they married, he had saved for an engagement ring – but never bought it because he gave the money away to a special offering. On one of his trips to America in the late 1960s, James was given some money and suddenly thought he would like to buy Sophia an engagement ring, though she was by then almost an old lady. When he put it on her finger, Sophia laughed and went off to make a cup of tea, "But she was pleased" said James. On another occasion, he saw a beautiful 'costume' the likes of which Sophia had never been able to afford. He brought it home for her, and when she wore it, he thought she looked like a queen.

The absences from Sophia had their effect on James. Whilst he had never pushed people away, he was an individualist, who rarely shared his hurts and disappointments. Now he grew warmer and more mellow and seemed to need people more. Of course there had always been some Ghanaians – like Pastor Safo and Pastor Paintsil – with whom James had a kind of father/son relationship, but once Sophia had returned to the UK, James used to spend more time with other people, and even invite friends, such as the Mills, to stay.

Although he had no children of his own, James always enjoyed being with them. In Ghana he would hug all the children – they loved him and flocked to him. Even when he was in his seventies, James used to get down on all fours under the table, chasing the four Mills children around. Back in Ireland, he took a particular interest in the little ones – buying sweets and taking delight in watching them grow up.

James said that the older he grew, the more he realised how lovely people are – that there is something beautiful in everyone if you only stop to look. "People long for the sort of relationship where they are appreciated and valued for who they are," he said. "If I lived my life all over again, I would love people more!" He once showed visitors a plaque on which was printed a Bible verse headed by the words "James: *truthful.*" Interestingly, he said, "I never liked my name, James. It is a cold name, a hard name. I prefer the name John – it is softer."

When he was not in Antrim, James was still travelling all over West Africa in his 70s and early 80s – quite a feat of endurance! Conditions were often primitive. One pastor took James to open a new church building in the north. The seats had only just received their final coat of cow-dung and, as if this were not enough, an insect bit James on the bottom. "I was horrified, but he didn't mind!" laughed the pastor. "He was always willing to live a simple life and not be served."

Some men would have cashed in on the prestige involved in leading such a successful Church. But Norman Barnes recalls an incident which shows how little James cared for such things. Norman was due to speak to a few hundred people at an assembly on the outskirts of Kumasi. Then someone else wanted him to speak to 5,000 at Kumasi's main civic hall. To Norman's horror, the small assembly said they would only relinquish Norman if James would come to speak to them. James had every right to take the large hall: instead he chose the small assembly.

During his last years in Ghana, James's travels meant anything from visiting assemblies and laying foundation stones of new church buildings, to speaking at conventions, at training seminars for leaders and on the radio. He contributed in terms of both finance and articles to new projects such as the magazine *Pentecost Fire.* As late as 1981, James brought Council the innovative idea that they should "get some retired Americans well-versed in agriculture and animal husbandry to train the youth in our schools." During this period, however, he was consciously trying to withdraw from many responsibilities, so that the African leaders had as much experience as possible of running the Church. Pastor Safo said that when he asked James's advice about something the answer would often be, "That's your look-out. Take your own decision!" James was making sure the leaders did not rely on him too heavily. Pastor Safo commented, "I saw he was training some of us to hold on like the eagle and not to fall."

Pastor J Egyir Paintsil had been Church secretary since 1952. The day to day running of the Church was in his capable hands while James was in the UK, and he was the obvious choice to succeed as chairman. Sadly however, just before the Council meeting in 1981, Pastor Paintsil fell ill and died. This left a leadership crisis. Pastor F. S. Safo was asked to step into the breach and take over as acting Church secretary. In April 1982 he became chairman. After 44 years superintending various churches in Ghana, James, at the age of 81, was at last able to retire. "The crux of the matter," James explained to the Church, "is that I feel I am far advanced in years and whereas young Ghanaians who are capable of handling the affairs of the Church are available, I need not deprive them of that opportunity."

James returned to Ghana just once during his retirement. In 1984, he went on a preaching tour with Pastor Safo. James said he enjoyed that trip. "We would travel maybe a hundred miles, preach twice, and return the same day. Only once did I feel unwell. I told Pastor Safo that he might have to preach, but when I stood, somehow the sermon was laid out in front of me – as though I was looking at the whole thing through a telescope – and I was able to preach well."

The last sermon James ever preached in Ghana was at the huge Sophia McKeown Temple in Labadi, and people had waited to hear him from four in the morning. James did not know it was to be his last sermon, but took a text he had never preached on before – 'Be ye followers of me, even as I also am of Christ.' (I Cor 11:1 AV) It is not every man who, in all humility, could say that at the end of his ministry.

"I found it easy to preach in Africa," James said. "I enjoyed my life there – we had such happy times ... conventions... meetings. I don't feel happy preaching here in the UK – I'm not educated, I'm just a bush man, really." In one sense, that was true. James became more African than English. He phrased things in a most unusual way, neither Irish or Scots, but African-English. (English is Ghana's official language and, just like American English, has developed a life of its own.)

James was not complimenting himself when he talked about being a bush man. Insecure in his lack of formal education, he failed to see that God turned his 'weakness' to a strength. James preached in Northern Ireland a few times. He thought he did badly: people who heard him remember it as quite outstanding. James had such a wide influence, bringing good news out of bad in Africa. He ended his days in another trouble spot which is full of religion, since Ballymena is a stronghold of Ian Paisley. His spoken testimony could have inspired thousands to go out trusting God as he did, yet few people outside West Africa have heard of him.

Occasionally, James was visited by a few British church leaders who come to learn from him. He could not understand this at all. His humility had reached an extreme. This spiritual giant of a man almost preferred not to recognise the work of God than to take any glory himself. When people come to ask him questions about how he built the Church in Africa, he would turn the conversation with questions about their church. As they left, he would astonish younger men by saying, in all sincerity, "I have learned a great deal from you this morning!"

When Sophia was 88, Eunice Addison came over to visit,

with her youngest daughter and two grand-daughters. Their gaiety filled the normally quiet bungalow. Sophia not only cooked huge meals but she was particularly anxious that the two children had eaten well and were happy – she insisted on doing all the washing up!

Soon after this visit, Sophia became prone to falling and broke her leg. Like most women, she would get in a state of panic before Christmas and on Christmas Eve, 1982, she turned suddenly to get something, tripped and fractured her good leg. James had never liked Christmas. He remembered too well one year when his mother had double pneumonia and his father looked after the family. The only present they had was a bit of fruit.

Sophia was admitted to hospital, but her heart began to fail. On January 27, 1983, she died and was buried in Portglenone, in the costume James had given her. Pride of place in Ballymena's Elim church hall is given to a huge and colourful *kente*[1] cloth, embroidered by the Ghanaians in memory of their 'beloved mother' who is missed by so many.

James had been used to prolonged absences from his wife. Still, her death affected him more than he expected – something within him seemed to die when she did, and, "It is not good for the man to be alone," he mourned. (Gen 2:18 NIV) Consistently James refused what seemed to many a logical step – to go and live with what had become his real family, in Ghana. The Executive of the Church and countless individuals did their utmost to persuade their beloved friend to return. There, community ties are so strong, it is almost unheard of for someone to live on their own and the Ghanaians could not understand why James chose to do this. They would have walked to the ends of the Earth for their

1 *Kente* is richly patterned cloth, hand-woven on narrow looms. It is worn by Ghanaian royalty – and today, by others who can afford it – on very special occasions.

'father' and very much wanted to honour him. Perhaps James was jealous of his independence, or perhaps he wanted the leaders in Ghana to stand fully on their own feet. Whatever his reasons, he obstinately refused to return.

In African culture, age is revered, but James hated growing old. One of his major regrets was that his mind could no longer concentrate. He lamented that it had become a major effort for him to spend four hours in prayer! It was not so much the exciting, public part of his ministry he missed. He was full of self-disappointment that he could no longer wait on God in the way he used to. In addition, because he read about Caleb and Moses, who were strong until the day they died, James felt he had failed when he succumbed to using a walking stick or hearing aid.

God did not leave James without anyone to look after him, however. Many of his large family still live in the Ballymena area – and then there was Pearl. It was Sophia who originally made friends with Pearl, the young mother who lived next door. Northern Ireland is a very religious place but Pearl seldom went to church. She had been horrified when she heard that her new neighbours were missionaries, but her daughter was only a toddler and had no such inhibitions. She just loved Sophia. Pearl soon realised she was never criticized for hanging out washing on a Sunday or pressurised about going to church. Pearl found a friend in the retired missionary and felt she could really talk to Sophia. One day, in Sophia's kitchen, Pearl came to know Jesus in a new way. She was filled with the Holy Spirit and her husband was drawn in too. They both regard Sophia as their spiritual mother. By the time their little girl had grown and married, the situation reversed and the couple became a life-line to James. Pearl looked after the needs of the increasingly frail old man who lived next door, with as much devotion as if he had been her own father.

James did not stop worrying about the future of the Church. He explained, "Now it is all so big, I fear others, whose work is not of the Spirit of God, might come in to spoil it and water down the good things sown." In 1987, the chairman of the Church of Pentecost died. Pastor Safo was just 55, a great man of God – strong enough and humble enough to lead the growing Church forward. His loss was tragic. James repeated again and again, "I have not another like Safo." There is no doubt that Pastor Safo's illness and death led to a shaking of the Church. The situation seemed dark because many of the other leaders, who as young men had pioneered with James, were due for retirement and the many younger pastors with vision, only had the potential to become front-line leaders in a few year's time. There seem to be relatively few leaders in their fifties who were of the calibre needed to hold together all the threads of this vast Church – young and old, mission and consolidation – men who were also capable of taking it on wherever God leads in the future.

After much prayer, in April 1988, Prophet M K Yeboah was appointed the new chairman of the Church, after being a regional head for many years. For two years he was the dean of the Bible school, where he was a real father to the students. He has the same spirit of humility as James and Pastor Safo had, and is so highly thought of that at least thirty children have been named after him. Brought up in the Presbyterian Church where his father was a minister, Martin Yeboah knew nothing about the new birth and Baptism of the Holy Spirit until he heard the full Gospel preached by some of James' men in 1947. He went on to enter the full-time ministry in 1951.

Prophet Yeboah wrote of the influence James had on him. "James became well known to me from when I entered the full-time ministry in 1951. I saw a real minister of the New Testament – a courageous, devoted, Spirit-filled man of God. I regard him as a loving spiritual father and leader. He is a man of discipline, prayer, faith, truth, sacrifice and simplicity. His first interest in life is the progress and welfare of the Lord's work, spiritually and numerically. He is a man of divine integrity, who loves holiness, truth and righteousness in all things. He hates nothing but sin and covetousness and loves nothing but truth and righteousness. He is indeed a shining example and a divine pattern – a man of God to all men of God."

In 1988, several retired from the seven-man Executive and were replaced by younger leaders – notably Pastor Ato Addison, the new general secretary. He has something of his mother Eunice Addison's spirit, and is also a very capable administrator.

If the Church has been through a crisis recently, it has been through many crises in the past and emerged the stronger. One of James's favourite verses was, "I will build my church, and the powers of death (lit. gates of Hades, Hell) shall not prevail against it." (Matthew 16:18 RSV). James McKeown did not build the Church of Pentecost. God did and that is why it has stood everything that has been hurled against it so far. In the past, much of its strength has come from its leader. James, Pastor Paintsil and Pastor Safo were giants among men – leaders of authority and integrity who kept a tight reign on the Church. Pastor Safo said before he died that the job of chairman had really grown too big for any one man to fulfil. Perhaps God is raising up men who will see leadership more in terms of a team. One thing is sure – the Church itself is a giant, and, like Samson, has daily choices to make. She will either follow God into greater things, or be robbed of the life that is in her.

Long before there was any talk of Prophet Yeboah being the new Chairman, I asked him about the future of the Church. He wrote in reply, "As the Church is not a human organisation, but God's, we have every hope and genuine conviction that as the Lord is on the throne, the promise made by Christ that the gates of Hell cannot prevail against the Church would be fulfilled. It is the keen and earnest desire of the Executive and the entire Church Presbytery to see that the Church would continue on the very sure foundation which is Christ our Lord and the only head of the Church which is His body. In doing so the leadership of the Church would not give chance to any human elements, desire and control in any form, but only to the leadership of the Holy Spirit and total obedience to the true genuine doctrines and faith of the early church of which we are a part."

God *is* building the Church, but he works through men. As Jayne Lindsell and I sat taking notes in the air-conditioned conference room of the Church of Pentecost's head office in Accra, a large photograph of James McKeown smiled down at us from the wall. As we witnessed all the varied activity going on around this nerve centre of the Church, and as we read through the minutes of the Council meetings over the years, we thought about the man through whom it had all started. Words some of our new Ghanaian friends had used seemed to hang in the air. "James did a big, big work in Africa. He set a good spirit and foundation and reputation..." In that very room, Eunice Addison had told us, "James came to minister life and those who were faithful have seen the fruit of what he came to minister. I say to the young pastors, 'Please put on the cloak James wore and greater things shall ye do.' " She added, "I want to see the Church riding high in holiness, truth and love!"

Ghana is a country which for many years has been full of missionaries – good, evangelical men and women, who made great sacrifices in order to see God's Kingdom extended in a foreign land. James's ministry was exceptionally successful. Why? His own reply to this question was typical of the man, "I was surprised when the Church grew – I thought I could have done better!"

James secret was that he won the African's trust. He never saw himself as white. He had no racial discrimination and there are not many people of whom that can be said. Then he found a way of communicating with the Africans in a way they understood. He went straight to the simple essentials – salvation from sin through the Cross and Baptism in the Spirit. Those things which were real to him, soon became real to them. As one Ghanaian friend put it, "James was sharp and had great impact on his hearers. Often other missionaries were cold and had no power."

A 'simple' farmer turned tram driver, James went to the mission field with no training. God had called him to do a new thing in the Gold Coast. He did not mix with other missionaries, nor did he benefit from the advice of academic institutions: he just listened to God and set things in motion accordingly. He knew his Bible and believed it, expecting God to work, expecting lives to change. James's clear mind had no preconceived ideas, so he was open to learn from the Holy Spirit. Prayer, in the sense of a two way conversation with God, must be one of the main keys to the man. Hearing God became so natural to him that he did not always realise where his wisdom came from. To James, many of the principles he applied were simply things that he had seen. Others would say they were profound truth and revelation from God.

For example, much has been written about the extraordinary church growth in South Korea. James had never heard of the 'Three Self Principles' of mission strategy. Originally propounded by a missionary to China, these were adopted in 1890 by the Presbyterians for use in their work in Korea. They stressed a quick transition from mission leadership to self-government in the national churches, as well as self-support and self-propagation. The one denomination which officially adopted these principles claims two thirds of all the Protestants in Korea today. The present Church of Pentecost leadership cite exactly the same three reasons for growth – self-government, self-propagation and self-support. It is clear that these principles came to them via James, who constantly gave away his authority and encouraged his leaders to take up responsibility. He trained them to be evangelists and insisted that they rely on God, and not the mission board back home, for finance. James said his principles did not come from Bible school nor from reading books: but that God often spoke to him when he looked at ordinary life. For example, the way James ran the church came out of his observations of farming families in Ireland.

Terry Muck, executive director of *Christianity Today* wrote an article about Pentecostalism[2]. In it he said, "Indigenous Pentecostal and charismatic churches in Africa and China have shown phenomenal increases. By targeting the poor and oppressed classes, allowing local church autonomy and encouraging the apostolic model of church planting, these churches have reaffirmed the Gospel's universal appeal." This was exactly what James did in the Gold Coast at a time when most churches were European and middle class in outlook. Terry Muck goes on to cite reasons for healthy growth such as worship, giving, prayer, Bible study, use of ministry gifts and 'antisecularism' – which he explains as living as if the supernatural really exists, and expecting the supernatural to invade the normal. This again is just the sort of Church James founded. The only thing which could perhaps be added to the list is his belief in the part women have to play.

In Ghana, James's own life and example must have caused the Church to grow. People saw Jesus in James – not just the 'surface water' of Christianity in the mind. When they recognised the truth of what James had in his own life, they wanted the same for themselves. James may have been just one man, but he was prepared to lay down his life to preach the Gospel. Like a seed that falls in the ground and dies, then is reborn into a new, vibrant dimension, James's life was to 'split rocks, and open prison doors'. The life in that 'seed' overcame any obstacle Satan or man could put in its way. It

2 *Christianity Today,* October 16th, 1987.

grew and bore fruit – James reproduced his own qualities in those who followed him; they became his spiritual children. He did all he could to encourage their growth and now they have gone on to see the Church grow into 'yet greater things'.

What sort of a man was this, that so many should follow him?

The very worst thing that could happen to James personally was to lose his sense of the peace of God's presence by stepping outside of God's will. Margaret Mills said that when she first knew James, "I used to sit stiff-backed at his table. I didn't want to make any sound that would ... I don't know... spoil the peace. It was strange. Whenever I took my children I would hold my breath throughout every meal – not that he would mind, but I thought he would mind, because he was a man of peace. Everything about him and Phia was peace. Their home was peaceful and I used to think that if I made a noise or did the wrong thing, I would spoil something for him and I never wanted that. He was someone very, very special."

James was a man of integrity, who insisted that everyone in the Church should live in a way that was pleasing to God. Because he would not let anyone get away with less, he set the Church on a good foundation. This was not legalism – James knew it is only Jesus who can do the greatest miracle of all and change people's lives.

Immediately recognisable as a man of authority, James would naturally take the lead in any situation – not because he threw his weight about, but because he was called and marked by God. Never one to use many words, when James spoke, everyone took notice.

James never felt he had any personal rights. To him the secret of a successful ministry was in taking up his cross and denying himself. If James demanded total dedication from others, it was because he had it himself. Single-minded about his task to the point of austerity, James was just not interested in externals. Ask him to describe a place, some food, or his house in Ghana and a one word answer was the best that could be expected. Possessions, food, comfort – all of these things meant very little to him. He even gave away most of his photographs.

James had a clear mind and his memory was always quite extraordinary. He would be able to recall in great detail dates, times and situations which everyone else had forgotten.

There was another side to this austere, powerful, saintly man. Despite the hurt and betrayal he had known, he was in many ways vulnerable and extraordinarily open. He did not stifle emotion, even though he made sure his will was always firmly in control of his actions. He was an overcomer, he could be uncompromising, but he did not grow hard in the process. His armour was the heavenly sort which does not keep *people* out – he radiated a love and a concern for all sorts of individuals.

The Ghanaians are open about their affection for James. They often refer to him as either 'our daddy' or 'our grandpa', and, when he is mentioned, say, "Oh James, we miss him!"

James's dry sense of humour belied the stern exterior. I arrived very early one morning and felt awkward. "Would you like to wait a little before I start the interview?" I asked. "I have not yet shaved," came his reply. I felt even worse. "And," he said, fixing me with a stern eye, "David has not shaved either." It was only as I looked up at David Mills' bushy beard that I realised I was being teased!

James was an interesting character, full of paradoxes. He was reserved, austere, upright, a man of single purpose and vision, of endurance and faithfulness, a man renowned because he not only spoke the truth, but lived by that same truth. It is not always the case that upright, austere, authority-figures inspire tremendous love: but James had an attractiveness which drew people to him. He had the mix of a peaceful heart and a fighting spirit, a love of good and a hatred of evil, a depth and a simplicity, an extraordinary humility combined with an extraordinary authority. His evident kindness and love could be as hard and uncompromising as diamond when necessary. He had a desire to serve, but an ability to rule. His selflessness and a longing to promote others combined with a sense of God's calling on his own life, so that he would never divert from the way he knew he must go. He might not always be a comfortable companion, but he would always have the best interests of others at heart. A visionary anchored in realism, above everything else he had the true missionary's love for souls who are perishing. That kind of love was the source of his single-mindedness.

Derek Poole, a housechurch leader in Northern Ireland, interviewed James, not long before Sophia died, and concluded the article he wrote with these words, "To most people in Northern Ireland, James McKeown would be totally unknown, but I believe the work he has done in Ghana will merit him that divine accolade, 'Well done, thou good and faithful servant.' After spending two hours in their presence, talking to James and being cared for by Sophia, I felt I wanted to sit at the man's feet and receive his blessing, but I was aware that it was now their turn to be served and given the honour due to them. May we as a younger generation learn how to honour such spiritual fathers and mothers, that our days also may be long in the land."[3]

Who knows how many heroes of faith, like James, are unnoticed? Yet we need heroes of this calibre to follow – people who will inspire us to reach out and prove God. Many of the principles James discovered could be used in other times, in other countries. Perhaps more importantly, if we learn from the way James followed Jesus, we will not become carbon copies of him – but we will see God's Kingdom

3 Derek Poole, "The Unknown Warrior", *Streams Magazine* Vol 1, no 1 (undated): p 16.

extended even through us. James's life shows that however ordinary our background, however small the beginnings or how big the obstacles which stand in our way – if we count the cost and follow God in single-minded obedience, we shall arrive at the vision he has given us. As we move out in faith, the very life of Jesus bursting within us will crack the rocks apart and the tiny, insignificant seed *we* have sown, may even change the face of nations.

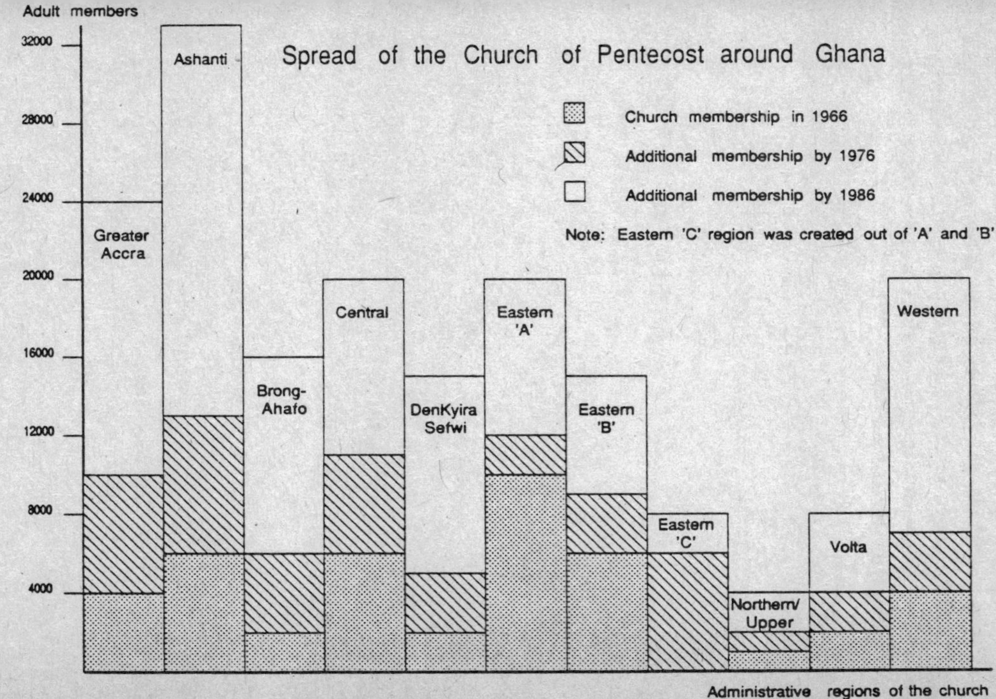

Spread of the Church of Pentecost around Ghana
Church membership in 1966
Additional membership by 1976
Additional membership by 1986
Note: Eastern 'C' region was created out of 'A' and 'B'
Adult members
32000
28000
24000
20000
16000
12000
8000
4000
Greater Accra
Ashanti
Brong-Ahafo
Central
DenKyira Sefwi
Eastern 'A'
Eastern 'B'
Eastern 'C'
Northern/ Upper
Volta
Western
Administrative regions of the church